Isn't That Enough?!
Musings of Motherhood and the Meaning of Life

Patty Ihm

Moorefield House Publishing

NILES, IL

Copyright © 2017 by **Patty Ihm**

All rights reserved. No part of this publication may be reproduced, distributed or transmitted in any form or by any means, without prior written permission.

Patty Ihm/Moorefield House Publishing
7948 N. Neva Ave.
Niles, IL 60714
www.moorefieldhousepublishing.com

Book Layout © 2017 BookDesignTemplates.com

Cover Art © 2017 Patty Kirk

Isn't That Enough?! / Patty Ihm. -- 1st ed.
ISBN 978-1-9470140-5-3

*To Mary Beth,
With love and gratitude ~
♡ Patty*

For my Tribe

Isn't That Enough?!
Musings of Motherhood and the Meaning of Life

Beginnings

(February 7, 2014)

In my reveries as far back as I can remember, I held a child in my arms. As a little girl, I spent collective chunks of time that would extend far beyond months and even years "housekeeping" and taking care of my baby dolls. Even as a high school girl, I would wander through the aisles of baby clothing at the department stores (sometimes with my dear friend, Marie, who somehow shared this passion), "window shopping," and looking forward, hopefully, to what would be many blessings one day. Unlike that of most of my peers, my ideal Saturday night was a long evening of babysitting a vast tribe of very young children (for perhaps seventy-five cents an hour, but I would have done it for nothing, to be sure).

Though I was certainly forced to watch horrifying and graphic films of crashes and matched to "student drive" through the mazes of traffic lights, pylons, triangle intersections and barriers, and even through a few near-death experiences alongside a perfect-driving football-player partner, what I remember most about driver's education was our simultaneous revelation, in the basement of St. Mary's Academy, that Marie and I were "almost twenty." We may have known what life was all about.

At two and a half times twenty, that is my burning question as I try my best to quiet the voices of my imminent middle age. Dan and I had married young, and I, at least, knew that we were matched for whatever our future would hold. I had looked forward to motherhood even from my own childhood so, when I discovered (at twenty-four, fresh out of graduate school) that my first baby was on the way, it was an easy decision to step away from my teaching position, so that I could take on the coveted role of mother at home.

Along with my young mother friends, I embraced the freedom of being home and spent many hours with my little sons knitting, baking, walking through the arboretum, sleeping soundly with a content little boy at my side, studying Waldorf education, playing in sand piles, making jams and canning tomatoes, exploring neighborhood parks, and--perhaps most memorably--whiling away hours at the Starry Sky Cafe. No wonder my young men cherish their coffee.

I look back on this time of immense peace with my children and think that there were many moments where I felt caretaking to be intense and challenging. It was then that I turned to those closest to me for support and reassurance. I often wondered what my future decades would hold, because my highest dreams directed me to those very days. One moment that will forever be with me: Caroline, a fellow mother whom I trusted with my heart and greatly admired, posed a question that had also been asked of her: "Isn't that enough?" I mean, what we were doing, and where we were; wasn't that enough?

There were some turns along the way. The little boys grew, and more children became part of our family. Dan and I became foster parents, and thus days of cookie baking and playing at the park often became swirls of angst, attempts to dodge misdirected anger, and shared grief over questions for which there really are no answers. The often-torrential chaos of my current days, though, is enough to assure me that right now, being here, is enough.

My high school English teacher once told me that when I fell and scraped my knee, I should first write about it, then bleed. My dog-eared purple journal that kept secrets beyond my teenage years has long since been discarded, but I have yet to forget the words of that wise man. Many falls later, I have finally decided to put pen to paper on a regular basis. I have a journey to share; one of motherhood, blessings, trials, passion, and the gifts of each given day. Isn't that enough?

The stars in my story are many; as our family has grown, so has my gratitude for the network of relatives, colleagues, and friends that have stood by my side. My husband Dan and I have been together for more than half our lives; as one we have navigated some roads that we may not have traveled alone. Though we may have waivered on some things, and it is still sometimes hard to decide where to go for dinner, one thing was certain: we knew that we would one day be parents.

We probably didn't, however, expect to be parents to nine children. That's a baseball team. Jonathan, our firstborn, taught me how to be a mother, even when I was nearly still a child myself. He gave reason and purpose to my days, and he quickly showed me how wise a little boy, and now, a young man, could be. James, a gentle, content little boy, came along three years later. Now strong with an adventurer's spirit, his childhood experiences have shaped him into who he has become. Kevin, our third little son, is still the wildly happy and active boy that kept me busy during his toddler years. Kind and independent, Kevin feels very deeply for those important to him.

Chae Young, not quite two years younger than Kevin, was born in Korea; we adopted her as an infant. There is much we will never know about what makes her who she is, but we do know that she was meant for us. When Chae Young was a small child, and as our four children grew, it became increasingly clear that there must be a higher power orchestrating our days. There was something about the energy and richness of the spirit of children; this may have been what led our family to foster care and to its inherent soul emptying trials and unimaginable joys.

Our little girl was in kindergarten when our thoughts of foster care became more than just quiet rumblings. Under the wing of a longtime foster parent and friend to our family, Dan and I made some phone calls and completed paperwork with the intention of opening our home to children. Right about that time, James, then ten years old, became very sick, and our plans were at least temporarily abandoned, as we were consumed by the needs of our son. Time marched along, James got better, and it was he that asked when the children would come. Over the course of twelve years, they came. We have been foster parents to eighteen children: some for hours, some for days, some for years, and some as forever inhabitants of

Ihm Home Farm.

Adrian came to us as a newborn, and upon his arrival I stopped working outside the home. His light shines as brightly as his anger is fierce. He is great motivation for writing, and his challenges are bigger than we may know. He has awakened a drive within many to keep searching, to keep looking for the answers.

Austin was already nearly an adult when we first met. He was a friend to our oldest son, Jonathan; they had common activities at the high school and shared what I perceived to be a mutual admiration for one another. Austin visited during a college break, and soon he began coming around more often. It seemed natural to have him at the kitchen table for holidays. At some point, Dan and I became "Dad" and "Mom," and he became our son. He moved abroad to do mission work, and when he came back for a visit, we officially adopted him as an adult.

Robin was just two days old when he joined our family. He has overcome many medical issues and serves as Adrian's arch rival and closest comrade, two years his junior, all wrapped in a smiling bundle of energy.

Our daughter Hope bridges the eight-and-a half-year age gap between Chae Young and Adrian. Hope has brought us, well, hope. Having experienced more in her early years than most of us will during our lifetimes, she has taught us much about courage and tenacity. As she grows toward her teenage years, her smiles, more frequent now, are rays of sunshine.

Our tiny caboose, Joey, is newly adopted into our family. I didn't expect to have a one-year-old at my half-century mark, but I cannot imagine where I, or anyone else in our family, would be without this little sprite. And that is how I feel about all of these children. They are true gifts, and there is a purpose to the presence of each of them within our home. We are all here for a reason, and one that we may never know, as long as we are here on this earth.

This is a story of our family, and, really, the story of many families. It's everyone's story, because we are all human. We all experience the depths of true emotion as we are led along the path of our days. And maybe, we all end up back where we first began.

The Most Beautiful Place on Earth

(February 14, 2014)

I always think of my college roommate on Valentine's Day. Today, she must have thought of me, because she sent me a little message about pizza. We shared a heart-shaped pizza at a restaurant on Greek Row, as college freshman on what, to many, is a day of great romance and candlelight.

Underneath the candles, I have found the real light.

Bridget and I were seated at a cozy table with love-struck couples visible at every angle. The pizza was perfect; the company, somehow, even better. The stars aligned to deliver me the perfect roommate (with whom over the years, I indulged in many more pizzas) when I was an innocent and vulnerable just-turned-eighteen-year-old. My perfect roommate had come to the university just days after suffering an unthinkable loss, one that made her among the most courageous people I have ever met. I am pretty sure that in my selfish oblivion, I had no idea the depth of her grief, and how she would comfort me over the years as she carried around her heavy suitcase, one that nobody could actually see. Those were such formative years for me; great blessings, indeed.

I want to fly, away from the part that hurts, but still into what I am now, never changing or passing with time.

Dan and I moved our young family back to DeKalb in 2000.

From my journal, dated 1-22-01: "As I was walking past the river on an afternoon... I again realized that DeKalb is the most beautiful place on earth. The Kish(waukee River), yet to be frozen, was running northerly, broken up in some spots by very white balls of smooth, snowy ice. All was still, and the university very, very quiet. Never, ever will there...be any regret for choosing this place. This is our home. The smallest reasons are the strongest confirmations."

I have always loved cookies. Bridget and I shared our passion for antiques: we would visit the dusty back rooms of whatever doors were open, it seemed, in search of Fiesta ware and vintage cookie jars.

I had ordered a plate of decorated cookies from the student catering building. On Valentine's Day, 2008, I ventured onto campus for the first time in perhaps over a year. With my three-month-old foster baby in tow, I collected the sparkly heart-shaped gems and stopped at the record store to share some of the treats with an old friend. The baby was safely in his seat (I think he was actually sleeping, which did not happen often in those early days) as I crossed the alley at the back of the parking lot, which edges the campus. I was taken aback by a student running, cell phone in hand, from the direction of the theater building and Cole Hall. As a wild animal runs to escape its hunter, so perhaps a dozen frantic-looking students followed suit of the first. Curious, I thought, as I pulled through the alley and drove down the street to get a coffee before picking up the elementary school set. Was this some sort of scavenger race? Maybe an acting class? It was, after all, near the theater building.

As I left the drive-through, latte in hand, my ears were flooded with sirens. First, one police car, then many. Rescue vehicles and frenzy filled my usually peaceful university. Reports were coming across the radio by now. I just needed to pick up my kids.

It wasn't until I was safely home that I realized how close I had been to the horrific, the absolutely unthinkable. Innocent people were breathing their last breaths as I passed by, as I was enjoying what may have been the most decadent butter cookie imaginable.

We are these people.

Clear the thoughts…rub your eyes…it's almost time to fly, fly.

Today, I am eternally grateful for my rich and deep blessings: my dear husband, my beloved children; my extended family; my deep and sustained friendships; my spirituality; my precious kitty, Juliet; my cookie jars; and, of course, pizza, heart-shaped or not.

TRUSTING WHO WE ARE MEANT TO BE

If I work too hard at trying to figure things out, the bits of meaning that come to me soon fall away. Just as the sun will rise, events will occur, sometimes with a shaking force, and sometimes slowly and over time, that shape my path, that create my story. Holding the notion that as time unfolds, the confused strings unravel to reveal wonder of their own, I can look back at the events on these pages and know that somehow, the person inside of me is who I will always be. Here are stories that have taught me to trust the design that has been set before. There is the story, among others, of a small child, of meeting the mystery of a childhood already in progress and embracing the uniqueness of this little one that has come to join us, with intriguing fanfare, for a tiny window of time. Though we may not know it, we are all bursting toward our true selves, righting our ships as we sink. My own experiences as an adolescent have helped me weather some deeper storms as my teenagers, too, explored the mystic wonder of the forbidden. Doing what you truly love is liberating to the soul; figuring out what that is may be where the challenge lies. The anxiety that comes with wondering whether you are doing the right thing, or when the state worker comes to call, isn't lessened by worry. No matter how others may perceive me, or how my path has curved along the way, I know that deep within, I am still here. I worried for my chickens, who are now producing an abundance of brown and blue-green eggs. I worried about the things that I couldn't know about, like what would happen if my chicken was actually a rooster, and how I would manage when my son moved away from home. I have been surprised by the beauty of a hummingbird on a day when my child's behavior was particularly trying. If we trust in what we cannot know, our experiences will, indeed, be our story.

A Bat in Winter

(March 14, 2014)

I can't sleep. It's not the time change. Not really. I never really can sleep; not in the way that the sleep informers would vise. Jonathan slept through the night at two months old. Once James came along, the co-sleeping, nursing, happy-even-at-two-in-the-morning second child, my nocturnal habits changed. James began to sleep through the night once Kevin arrived a bit more than three years later, and then things got a little out of hand with the subsequent children, most of whom had very different ideas for what happens during the deep hours of darkness.

It's not always the children, or swirling thoughts associated therein, that interrupt or forbid my sleep. Sometimes, it's bats. Years ago, one of my foster daughters informed me that she was "part bat." I cannot speak to the truth of that statement, because that very night, there was a bat circling my bedroom. I don't remember whose turn it was to trap this one, but by the time we released it and I ventured down the hall to check the children, my sweet girl was sleeping peacefully. I am not sure if she reentered through a crack in the wall, or if it was just a coincidence, and I will never know.

At our old house by the university, we once spotted a bat in the bathtub. One of the boys (probably close to teenage at the time) had been using the bathroom earlier. "Oh, that? I thought it was a piece of poop."

Which would not, actually, be all that odd in our home. I like using something called "Black Soap" for my black children. It seems to be quite beneficial for their skin. In the chaos of boats, overzealous splashing, and the fight for who "gets out first," I left some Black Soap on the edge of the tub. It was, of course, identified as poop but not wiped up. I am actually grateful that it wasn't, though, because Black Soap is not very easy to come by.

"It is only with the heart that one can see rightly. What is essential is invisible to the eye."

That's a quote from Antoine de St.-Exupery's timeless classic, "The Little Prince," which happens to be my favorite book, as it was long before most of my life began happening to me. I am reminded of this message every time a new child comes to my home. We are all regular people. We all have a story. We can all look in the mirror and, over time, begin to see what we stand for. The smallest, most fragile child is a person whose life has deep meaning.

If I open my mouth, if I speak my mind, will this…can this…change the outcome of a given situation? Will it be better or worse? Will we even know? There are times when we are not up to the task. Not right now. Does that mean that we will ever be? What if she really is a bat? We won't ever know that, because her time with us was just a matter of days. What if I really am a bat?

Maybe the time change was keeping me from sleep. Maybe it was our little son who, at four, is wakeful at times each night, and who crawled into our bed to wedge his elbows and heels into our backs. Scratching, flapping, and a little breeze. A bat. In winter. Wherever you are, little girl, I hope you are happy. You have so much to share.

A Badass Pollyanna of Sorts

(March 27, 2014)

She's a vision of a cat. That's not a real cat, is it? Yes, yes, it is. How can that actually be a cat? She is so... perfect. And up on the counter, actually up on the toaster, she sits. As quickly as she is redirected from the forbidden spot, up jumps Juliet, back to her berth. Oblivious even to the squirt bottle, she pokes her pug nose skyward and cozies up as close as she can to the crock pot, likely unaware of the cream cheese tortellini within. Juliet, our dear Himalayan Persian, is uncivilized. Sweet as pie, and as rebellious as Johnny Rotten.

When I let baby Jonathan loose to crawl about his uncle's college apartment floor, he ate a glow-in-the-dark star. Though it worried me at the time, that incident may have had some impact on his developing mind. Most people have not eaten glow-in-the-dark stars. And most people are not as bright as Jonathan.

From a place deep within, we are all bursting toward our true selves. And try as we might, it seems we cannot really alter the soul essence of who someone is. I'm never going to like pimentos; I am never going to learn to ballroom dance; I will never not be awkward speaking in front of people; and I am most certainly not going to change the minds of my children by imposing my views upon them. Though what I say or do might possibly have an influence on another person's thoughts or actions, the heart of another being is independent of my perceptions and projections. I will forever be burdened with trying to do what I think is the right thing (though actually it may not be), and with the feelings of guilt and anxiety that make me wonder whether my actions were justified.

I believe in people. I have witnessed true, course-changing, life-altering, behavior in others. Many times I have reached out, and a good number of those times I have been shamed, rejected, or made to feel less than whole. And I wonder if I am perceived, to those people, as I feel inside…as I am inside.

There was a doll that I wanted with a fervor as a little girl: Joey, the anatomically correct likeness of Archie Bunker's grandson. When I finally opened the box and disrobed the baby, I felt a sense of regret. I felt like I shouldn't have that doll at all. As my little son would say, I felt like it was inappropriate. I wonder why I had wanted it so badly.

A game of telephone at a grade school sleepover: a circle made of a dozen wide-eyed, giggly girls, whispering "the message" in turn to the person to the left. I vividly remember pretending that I didn't understand and eventually lost my turn; I was pretty sure I wasn't allowed to say those bad words!

There is an unsung splendor, a mystic wonder in the forbidden. It is up to us to sort out the feelings borne from our choices. Some seem worth the risk.

I was sent home for wearing navy blue corduroy walking shorts (clad with mini green whales); this resulted in the only detention I remember from high school. I wanted to wear my new shorts, and I knew it was against the rules. Chewing gum was strictly forbidden at the Catholic high school. A devil among angels, I found a way to hide my Wrigley's Spearmint in my cheek so no one suspected a thing.

The rebellion was in full swing in college. I was gifted (honestly) a fake ID by a sorority sister that had been mugged. Not once did I have to grovel to gain entry to The Jungle on New Wave Night; I was handed my golden ticket by someone who had recovered her stolen identification. I mastered her signature and flashed my prize with confidence on those Tuesday nights. When the police raided the bar (looking for underage entrants), we scurried to stack ourselves in the bathroom stall until the coast was clear. Always with great relief, I would return to my club soda. I was not about to order alcohol from the bar, but I am pretty sure I did not consider the idea that possessing a fake ID was likely a higher crime.

I had a rare college job that was more of a haven than a place of employment. I worked at a record store. The smell of Gonesh incense ($1.87/pack) still lingers in my soul, to be sure. I sat up on the counter, with no shoes on, and ate croissant sandwiches with Muenster cheese and mustard (from the deli next door) while selling records to people. I'm not sure if I sat on the counter in front of the boss; I wonder what, if anything, he would have had to say about that. Doing what you truly love is liberating to the soul.

Most of my days are spent in jeans and nondescript shirts, probably because my primary job is to wipe stuff. I do, though, have a long-standing love for vintage clothing and well worn, comfortable pink things. On one of my trips home from college, my dad eyed me quizzically and referred to me as "Laura Ashley to ash pit." But it was still me on the inside, just the same.

I woke a few mornings ago to a collaboration of snoring and wheezing in the bed beside me. The wheezing, at least, came from the four-year-old bedfellow who, until his adoption was finalized, was not supposed to sleep in our bed. So many nights in his young life, this rule was broken as we, his foster parents, kept vigil and shifted him in his dreams to open his airway, so he would not breathe his last breath. Sometimes, we have to make choices that hardly seem like choices at all.

As the song goes, I have been encouraging my girls to speak bravely and honestly. This has, on occasion, backfired into a license for tongue whipping episodes of talking back, certainly not what I had intended with my plea. I hope, though, that they understand that they have voices which deserve to be heard. As I have approached middle age and as my passions dictate, I have begun to practice saying what is on my mind. Though a quiet voice can speak volumes, there is a place for words; words that, when spoken, reveal some level of injustice. I walked away from a job when the ethical issues overshadowed my purpose as a teacher. If you cannot make it right with yourself, then perhaps it is not right for you.

When the time comes that you meet your one true love, you fall deeply for how that person lives his or her life. We fall again, with each of our children, and all of their differences. My babies come to me from many different places. I cannot be sure if any of them, with the exception of Jonathan, has a glow-in-the-dark star burning within. I am trying to embrace the choices and the behaviors, no matter how bright or nonsensical they seem. We are all here, shoes or not, pop music or punk rock, jumping onto the kitchen counter to bask in the warmth of the crock pot (or parking oneself on the counter of the record store back in the day) baring our vulnerable souls, standing for what we believe.

I wonder if Juliet will ever learn her boundaries. And I wonder if she did, would part of her unique charm be lost in the compliance? And through our struggles, confusion, embarrassment, and rebellion, the little bits of magic that shine through bring us to realize that allowing ourselves to be who we are…who we always have been…is, after all, the right thing to do.

Mercy

(January 6, 2016)

There's nothing like an impending monitoring visit from the state's licensing worker to motivate me to clean my toilets. I have long since stopped worrying about most of the details that swirled through my brain in a jumbled checklist during our early years of fostering, but, still today, the toilets have to be clean before I can open the door for what is hardly a white glove inspection. We have had other people's precious children in and out of our home for eleven years now, but someone still comes to check up on us every six months because, as I so often tell my children for so many things, "it's the rule."

All nine of my kids were here this Christmas, and in the aftermath, there's plenty of work left for me. And when the little one is sleeping and the house is peaceful, I actually like to clean my house. Even the toilets.

With my vinegar-and-water rag in hand, I studied what was before me in the downstairs bathroom, which also happens to be a laundry room: thick, weathered pine trim defines the opening to a closet under the stairs. The smell inside that secret space, though not clearly definable, had been off-putting enough when we first moved in that I had to hang a basket of my best incense to make it as inviting as the century-old light fixture mounted proudly to an inside wall of this closet. As my rag met the edge of the pine, I was drawn to hints of yellow-orange, which almost seemed to cry out to beg my awareness. In that moment, I did see the sun. Our farmhouse was built in 1877. Surely the washy beige, almost colorless wall, and the sunnier shade of a yesterday which can barely be determined, are not the only two colors to have graced these bathroom walls. More than likely, there were many, many more. More than likely, too, is that this was something other than a bathroom at some point in history.

It has been almost a year since I decided to let my hair dread. If I had known that this journey would involve so much crazy looping and a really wild, tangled mess on most days for upwards of a year, two, or three, I doubt I would have stuck with it. I would have combed it out and continued to wish for what will, as I know now, take years to mature. Instead, I have forged on, embracing the knots, and tying my hair back when I have to go somewhere or clean something (or when a licensing worker is coming to my house). I have decided to let this happen, to release control, because in the end, I am pretty sure that I am not in control anyway. We have to start somewhere.

I wonder, too, had Dan and I known that so many years into standing up for our kids, hauling files and articles to the schools, keeping vigil through the night, doing our best to be consistent when we needed to and flexible when we could…explaining, begging, tolerating the same verbal rants over and again, being pelted by words which imply that this is all our fault, feeling fragile and vulnerable in our own home, and crying millions of tears, all in hopes of washing away the layers of paint, of pain, that cover, even hide, the time underneath…the years of life lived…would we have had the courage to begin this journey?

My kids have opened up the inside of my soul, and in some ways I know that time has painted over much of what I used to be.

My active little son tries to eat soap and lotion with the same passion his brother had, and occasionally, at six, still has. I thought I might be clever and have at least five seconds of peace in the bathroom yesterday, so I put a safety lock on the low cabinet with the extra body wash and bars of Irish Spring. Once he realized he couldn't open the door, he took a few Frankenstein-style steps in front of the toilet (where I sat) and managed to pull down the makeshift curtain (which was actually a Winnie-the Pooh crib sheet), exposing me in all my vulnerability to anyone that decided to drive down our country road. At least it's not well-traveled.

It's still me inside. And unless you know me, you might not really know me. I might not really know my kids; I may never get to see their brightest suns. There's much more to them, and to me, than anyone may ever know. Yet I am at their mercy, as they are at mine.

The licensing worker was in and out of our home pretty quickly that day; we are good for another six months. I wonder if he would have noticed if my toilets hadn't been clean. As I gathered the basket of laundry to take upstairs, I noticed my neatly folded underwear, two pair, on the laundry table, and I wondered if the state worker, too, had seen them. At least they were clean.

Chicken Anxiety

(February 23, 2016)

In twenty days, ten two-day-old chickens will be waiting for me at the local feed store. My chickens, highly touted and long awaited, will be coming home. They will lay fresh eggs for our family, they will serve as my partners in the garden, and they will be the realization of my first vision for Ihm Home Farm.

My teeth would begin to ache when the hour approached. It was nearly impossible to pay attention to Sister Elizabeth's geometry lesson, however riveting it may have been, as my mind bumbled along images of note cards… reciting words that I had spent into the wee morning hours committing to memory for next period's sophomore speech class.

I have never been comfortable talking in front of a crowd of people. Thirty uniform-clad teenagers, attention at half-mast, and one robust nun who counted points off for every stutter or "um," was certainly considered a crowd as I stood at the front of the class to face my fears. Knowing my subject made my presentation easier but did nothing to calm my nerves, quiet my shakes, or make me enjoy high school speech.

For many years I have been dreaming of chickens free ranging on our property. Now, the chickens are on the way, and with this vision has come "chicken anxiety."

The familiar current began running through my body as the caller ID proclaimed "State of Illinois." This would likely mean one thing: a new foster placement. All of the things that I had been meaning to accomplish or prepare "in case" loomed before me as one unattainable "to-do" list. I forgot to get the lice remedy after the last one ran out, we have no more bananas, I was going to paint the dresser in the girls' room.... I am overwhelmed with the thought of trying to pull things together for a potential new beginning. I could cross off a few things from my list if only I could stop pacing.

My oldest son, Jonathan, who has pretty much always been far wiser than me, once said that anxiety can serve us well; it can keep us motivated. But will it help me do right by my little flock?

I am worried about my chickens. I am having trouble deciding which feeder to use, and whether I should use sand or pine shavings on the coop floor. What if I am not able to keep it clean enough, and what if the eggs could make my friends or family sick? Should I feed my new pullets medicated starter feed? What if they get sick? What if something gets in the coop? What if they get mites? Do I need to clean my boots each time I visit the op? What if my chickens eat the wild bird seed? What if they fight among themselves? Oh, wait; I think I may be able to handle that one...

As I have worried myself through my years of fostering, I know that I now feel better equipped to understand and take on situations that I may have felt differently about without some practical experience, and without having lived through some pretty unsettling scenarios. Now I understand that the eight-year-old who is relieving herself anywhere but the toilet may be controlling the one thing that she actually can control. I understand that the stash of candy wrappers and empty juice boxes shoved forgetfully out of sight between the wall and the bed are a function of a past where there may not have been enough to eat. I know that investigations are part of this journey. I understand, too, that I may never be the first best mom to some of my children, and that trust, in the world of foster care, is never a given.

Stacks of chicken books, trips to the feed store, advice from chicken-keeping friends, hours of perusing the online chicken group; all of these have given me much to ponder. And still, there is the anxiety.

This late winter, two of my dear, longtime friends lost chickens to predators. They adored their chickens and, I know, did their very best to care for them every day. Sometimes, though, there are detours. The bus stops where you didn't plan to get off. The worrying that we do steals away our gifts of this given moment.

Both of my friends are still keeping chickens. I made it through my high school speech class, though I am still uncomfortable in front of a crowd. We have even been through an investigation and have come out on the other side. Though there is much that I do not understand about the children that come to stay with us, I can appreciate that their behaviors have meaning, and that they have come to teach me, if I am open to learn.

I hope my chickens will be able to tell how happy I am to welcome them home. They will be scared, confused, and maybe even feisty. But they will be mine to care for, for however long. I hope that by the time I have gathered my first few eggs, my chicken anxiety will have subsided. At least, that is, until I begin to worry about how I will tend to them in winter.

If I don't pick up my chickens in twenty days, I will never know what chicken keeping will bring. I will only continue to dream of the day that hens would populate my yard. If I let my fears stand in the way, I will miss the moment. If we come to the table with what we have, I do believe that must be better than staying behind.

I am keeping a good thought for my chickens and all those who have gone before, for students that have anxiety about giving speeches, for all of the children waiting to know what their futures hold, and for all of our fears in hopes that they may become our opportunities.

Things We Don't Know

(May 9, 2016)

There must have been something under Kevin's basket of folded laundry. It was tipped enough that each time I tossed the pair of socks into the pile, it bounced out and landed on the floor. I gave up after a while. I thought about a game at a tucked-away amusement park that we had discovered on a family vacation during a camping trip to the western states. If you played one of the games long enough, you just might figure out the trick that would lead you to a poly-stuffed monkey with an obscurely screen-printed face, this animal that you would carry proudly on your shoulders as you made your way to the Tilt-A-Whirl or the Himalaya as onlookers coveted such a grand carnival prize. I did not, though, know the trick to getting the socks to stay in the basket on this day. I had to pick them up from the floor, all the while wondering if this would be the last time I matched this boy's socks before he moved to his own place.

I had three placement calls from the child welfare agency last week: one for a fifteen-year-old girl, one for a twelve-year-old boy, and one for a five-year-old boy. Though we are over our capacity with a sibling waiver, these calls always leave me feeling a bit hollow, almost powerless to the grip of the unknown. Three young lives disrupted and uncertain...what is going to happen to these children?

Tending my chickens has become a form of therapy for me, right beside my longtime love of gardening and, more recently, the defining of my emotions through writing. I visit the chickens several times each day, to take care of them; to watch them scurry with curiosity toward me as I open the run to lure them outside with this morning's treat: celery, leftover coffee cake, sunflower seeds, or a pinch of basil; to clean under the perches and to toss some fresh pine shavings into the coop. They are no longer just steps away from me at all times. They are growing, they have transitioned to their outside hen house, and soon I will be checking the nest boxes for the first prized egg. Much of the winter had been devoted to studying about chickens, and I knew my hens would teach me what I needed to know along the way. I wanted to be prepared. I would start with all girl chickens, for roosters will fertilize the eggs and can cause trouble, even becoming aggressive to their human caregivers. Heaven knows we have enough combative behavior here at the farm. We don't need the chickens chiming in.

My little boy has grown up. He is looking to move to an apartment with friends. I know; that is what is supposed to happen. It will hardly be an empty nest when he leaves the farm, with five children still at home, and, of course, ten chickens in the backyard. I won't be lonely, but I will be lonely for him. I will be lonely for those long ago days, when we would lay in the grass and look at the stars on a clear night, when I didn't have to think about such uncertainties.

And then the day came when we could no longer deny that Wendy...Wendell...was a rooster. From our early brooder days, Robin had noticed, "Wendy was the leader." My intuitive six-year-old chicken helper had known all along. The bossy behavior, the bright red comb, the distinctive ruffly feathering, and the way he carried himself were adding up to punctuate my worries. Suggestions poured in. We could sell him. We could give him away. We could break his neck. We could eat him. We could let him out to become prey to the visiting hawk. Or, we could keep him. He could protect his flock from predators. And we would have fertilized eggs. Nearly every morning, Wendell is first to emerge through the chicken door. Some might say that he is surveying the territory for safety, but I like to think Wendell wants to be first in line for his breakfast treat.

The little boy's resilience, if only for this day, astounded me. He read the street signs as we drove through the country, into the city, and back to my house again. I wondered if he, at seven years old, had learned to read so well to keep his mind from some of the less comprehensible things in his life. He stayed with me just for the day. I was looking after him because his foster family (where he had been for such a short time that he was not yet enrolled in school) had to attend an out-of-town funeral. Another family had kept him on the weekend, and he was with yet a different caregiver until the first family returned from out of town. He came to me on this day, though, while his third caregiver was at work. He wanted me to play checkers with him, and he asked if he could have peanut butter pie, a Whopper, and chicken fries from Burger King. He also wanted me to take him to the park. We spent eight hours together that day, and he was pleasant company. I marveled at his stoic presence in the midst of such chaos, such transition, and such uncertainty.

"Here. I know how to do that."

I gave him a handful of chicken feed. He tossed it with a strong, confident motion, which led me to believe that he had grown up an apprentice to a chicken keeper.

"You've done this before?" I asked.

"No. But I watched them do it on TV. You know, farmers. Can I have a bag of popcorn, please?"

He asked if he could stay with me that night. Of course he couldn't; we are at capacity, and I was only watching him for the day. I wonder where he is now. I wonder how he could possibly be okay. I bet he knew how to win the carnival prize, and I hope he did.

The day will come when Kevin will have the keys to his new place. I am better off not knowing when that will be. My little visiting friend found comfort and meaning in his own curiosity during what was certainly the most turbulent time of his life. In our time together, he has reminded me to be aware of the path, to forge ahead and to trust what we know, even if it means a little detour, and always, always, be open to learn. Those fertilized eggs are going to taste just fine.

Lessons from Popeye and the Hummingbird

(June 13, 2016)

I overheard her telling someone that nothing could really hurt her. When you have been broken more times than the number of years you have lived, and when your heart has been shattered into a million tiny pieces, you already know the worst kinds of hurt. What more could there possibly be that you have yet to endure? She collected what fragments she could in the aftermath of brokenness, and she hurled them at anyone that stood in her way. Those who were closest to her, those who were in the line of fire, felt the deepest hurt. This hurt, though, was a hundred million times softer than the hurt, than the grief that had swallowed her as Jonah in the belly of the whale, with no clear route to escape.

We were sometimes allowed to stay up until ten o'clock on Friday nights. I remember being an early riser as a young child, and I could probably have been the first to the television on Saturday mornings even if I had been last to bed the night before. I did not, though, find the charm in most cartoons. My mind would drift, and I would not really understand what was happening on the screen. I think I still have that going today, for more than just cartoons. I did, though enjoy the Popeye show. Olive Oyl was tall and skinny, and I admired the skirts that she wore. I liked Sweet Pea, the baby in his little sleeper, best of all. And I heard Popeye's message loudly and clearly: eat spinach, for it will make you strong. I really like spinach, and I owe it all to Popeye. These days, I can eat fresh spinach by the handful from my garden. And I am still trying to find my strength.

If you believe something, it's closer to happening than if you don't. The hope is there, pulsing in its existence. My babies, my sons who are now grown men, believed in me, because I gave them life. I was what they knew, and they trusted me, even without having a soft place to land. They looked to me to be there for them, and they needed me, even in my own frailty, when inside I was full of fear. It has not been the same for those children; my children who have come to me bearing the weight of another life lived. They are skeptical. They test and challenge. They do not believe. They make me question my own truth, strength, and integrity. My hands shake, blood rushes through my legs, and I am overcome by my own acts of hyper vigilance which cause me to stay awake, wide-eyed, tears flowing, fearing the cobra as I anticipate the nearly undetectable sound of the coil and wonder when the next strike will be.

I wonder, too, how long it will take for her to trust, to believe, and if she even ever will. She certainly is strong, but it isn't from eating spinach. Well, there is a little spinach in our recipe for tortellini soup. But that isn't what Popeye had in mind. Time and again, she is overwhelmed by her own conflict and disbelief.

Two times before, I fancied hummingbirds as backyard visitors. I prepared the nectar, hung the feeders, and waited for something that wouldn't happen. Once I even forgot about the nectar for a long while, only to remember when I discovered a sticky mess and a trail of ants where my dreams of a magical little bird had been waiting to manifest. Earlier this month, I was shopping for chicken feed when I chanced upon a pretty little red glass, vintage-looking feeder. It was my message to try again, though I needed, first, to find my faith that they would one day come. We chose a spot just outside the kitchen window, and Dan hung the feeder with a re-purposed candelabra that we had found behind the barn. It looked lovely, just as it was. I knew it would take time, and I would try to remember to refill the nectar this time.

Maybe it's the collective spinach that you eat, over years and years, that gives you the kind of strength that you need to believe. More than likely, though, it's time, patience, a sense of purpose, and knowing that you are truly, deeply loved that will make the difference in the end. When all the fight is gone, battle-weary and vulnerable, we turn to our Maker, knowing that this is what He had in mind for us all along.

My shoulder stung where my embattled eight-year-old had sunk his frustration and his fingernails hard into my flesh in the wake of brotherly combat. "It's okay. We're okay." That was all I had to offer as I walked away from the heap of his body. All his fight had gone out, at least for this moment. As I went to find my iced tea, something caught my attention outside the kitchen window. It had come just for me, in that moment, and with a message to deliver. Looking tentative and almost disheveled, the tiny gray hummingbird darted off as quickly as it had come. But it came, and with it followed a whole new kind of hope.

It's not up to us. It's not our plan, or even our time. For Jonah, whose name, I learned, means "dove," a peaceful bird that frequents our feeders at the farm, the urge to flee was not enough to keep him from the path that was intended solely as his. We can't hide from ourselves, from our own truths, and from what is in store for us. I guess we all just need a vision, a little tenacity, our fair share of spinach, and maybe some help believing that someone will keep returning to catch us along the way.

****

We all have a story. As our stories take shape, there are so many pages left untold. Some, we will never understand or even know. My sweet bat girl stayed with our family until she could be moved to live with her sister, in their hometown. I sent a few little plastic animals to her through her caseworker; she had spent time in the sand pile in our backyard creating adventures for these animals, and I thought she might enjoy some new adventures one day, in her new surroundings. I didn't hear back from her, but I hadn't expected to.

With my own teenager's antics in full swing, I felt compelled to share that I, too, had crossed some lines while growing up: I even told them about my fake ID. I wonder if this disclosure made me more vulnerable and gave them more ammunition to justify their own "crimes," or whether, as was my intention, it highlighted our common, albeit devious, human behavior.

We are who we are. Though with Joey's recent adoption we no longer have any foster children in our home, we will probably commit to renewing our license when the time comes next spring.

We will sign up for four more years of caseworker visits, house inspections, and vulnerability. We will continue to leave the door open because, without a doubt, part of our story is yet to be written.

After much consideration, I chose to go with pine shavings for the chicken coop. This was a good decision, as bales are readily available at the feed store for just a few dollars. Every day, there are certain chicken rituals to be completed; I look forward to the peace that it provides me to open the coop door in the early morning, to clean the roosts and nest boxes, to refill the feeder and waterers, and to take just a few minutes to check in with my beloved birds. The routine has eased my anxiety. I can care for chickens. There are new things now, though, that bring me worry. If I let them range free around the property, will they be safe? Will they fall prey to the hawk that sometimes circles overhead? They have learned to return to the coop at dusk, and, thus far, they seem to be enjoying their freedom as they poke around the herb garden and sneak food from the barn cats' bowl.

Wendell, our rooster, perches on the porch rail and crows with abandon. He does his best to protect his flock, even to the point of stirring fear in my little ones, just as we, as parents, want to keep our children safely under our wings. Kevin, along with the free-spirited cloud of happiness that tries to contain him, has moved out on his own now, and, though he comes around often, his presence at the farm is deeply missed. I sometimes wonder if Wendell might be calling for our boy when he crows.

I had a lush crop of spinach this year, with plenty to share with visitors and friends. When the days were consistently warmer, though, the spinach seemed to bolt to bitterness nearly overnight, offering only leaves that were no longer salad worthy. There will be moments: triggers that catch us by surprise. The spent spinach went first to be picked over by the chickens and then to the compost pile. I planted two small rows of lettuce to fill the barren corner of the garden as the weather has turned, and as a last offering before the soil will be prepared for the next season.

As for the hummingbird, it appears outside my kitchen window almost on a regular basis. Perhaps it is not the same little bird that had first visited. It looks more graceful, suspended at the feeder, with feathers of a brighter, more magical palette. I like to believe that it is the very same hummingbird that first discovered the nectar; I like to believe that it has grown richer, more graceful, and more beautiful with each passing day.

ACCEPTING WHAT IS BEYOND OUR CONTROL

"Parenting is hard." Those are words shared by more than just a few wise friends and words that I, too, have offered to others as I had come to realize the truth and magnitude of that simple line. Sometimes, the challenges seem insurmountable, so far beyond our control that we may wonder how we will make it to the other side. Somehow, though, through the tears, suffering, and struggles, we always do. Often, I had thought that the depth of my love and the strength of my devotion would be enough, that it should be enough. I learned, though, that this cannot always be true. I didn't think it could be so hard, or that I would need to let so much go in order to let in the good.

I didn't think that when my love would not be enough to heal, that my child would need a level of help that I could not offer. I couldn't know that the pain of separation could hold such power, and that we would forge together, however challenging, a new vision for our future. These are tales of inpatient psychiatric hospital stays and their effects on the whole family; lessons in embracing the idiosyncrasies of others; stories about separating yourself from those that you love to the greatest depths; and words of acceptance that though endings are hard, the promise of tomorrow can be enough. Through our collective disappointments and defeat, we let go of today, of what we cannot control, so that we may see the new sunrise, so that we may find the meaning in the brokenness and the gifts in the rebuilding.

The Journey
(November 16, 2014)

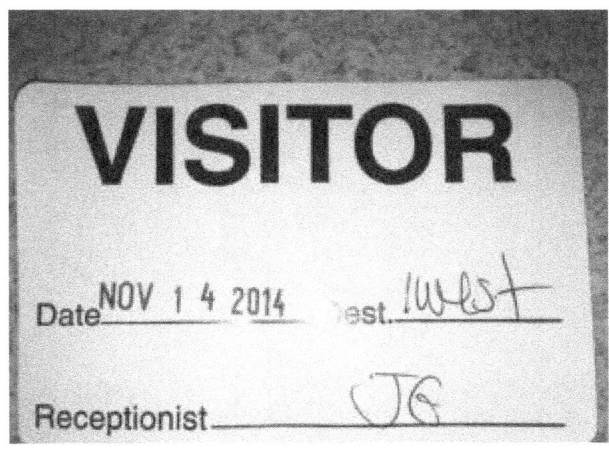

"Looks like Randy got some new shoes!"

Randy, a child of perhaps eight or nine, stuffed into gray sweatpants that would have actually fit someone at least thirty pounds lighter, was unintentionally mooning those of us in the adjacent visiting room as he parked himself on the polished tile floor like a monument in front of the reception desk. I am not sure if he was wearing socks, but he was doing his best to lace the high-top gym shoes, which were certainly new, with great fanfare. Another boy stared at Randy and paced around the monument a time or two. This boy had an unusual red streak-type mark traversing one side of his face; it appeared to be either a marking pen accident from several showers earlier, or the result of losing a physical battle of some sort. I never did see Randy's face, but I imagined that it must have reflected an eager anticipation at the prospect of actually being allowed on the other side of the door of One West, which had been his holding tank for his "five-day," or however long it had taken him to demonstrate the type of behavior necessary to be released to the outside world once again.

"Randy is going home," Adrian said, matter-of-factly. While he didn't seem especially happy for Randy, neither did he seem to be wishing that he was the boy in his place. He just wanted to play with the Duplo blocks.

An hour earlier, I had dropped Robin off in Elmhurst to spend the morning with my dear friend, Susanne. Our families had lived on the same street when Dan and I were first married. We had been first-time mothers together, with those babies and even their little brothers now in graduate school and college. Hours we spent on park benches and in the Starry Sky, our best coffee shop, eating lemon shortbread and never even considering that those days would one day be mere memories. Driving down York Road, I noticed a band of little Catholic girls in uniform skirts and knee socks; they were outside but contained within a chain-link fence. It must have been recess. One kicked a soccer ball toward a net as several others scrambled to block the kick, and a few others huddled together near the fence. I imagined them sharing secrets and giggling in high pitches. As I approached the center of town, I dared not drive down Clinton Avenue for worry that my tears might distort my vision, and I might not make it to Adrian. I would see one-year-old Jonathan climbing on his Little Tykes slide in the front yard, early in the evening as we waited for Dan to come up the street with his briefcase. I would see the front porch where I hung Christmas lights for the first time as an adult, and where I would sit, into the dark hours of the early morning, and watch the snowfall while I wrote my hopes and visions in my purple journal. It would be too much to bear, going back to those simple days, as I would know that my just-turned-seven year-old is behind lock and key, with no windows at all, certainly without sparkling Christmas lights, with nobody to pull the covers over him each night, and with nobody to wish his fears away.

As I drove nearer to the hospital, behind a foreboding darkish iron gate there was a sprawling cemetery with gravestones sprinkled with artificial flowers in sun-faded colors that had probably been, at one time, lovely and cheerful. I wondered how many people had driven by that day without actually noticing it, as I am sure I did every time before this one.

"Oh, Risperdal. Do you know one of the side effects of Risperdal?"

It was the boy with the red streak. He must have overheard the doctor talking with me about Adrian's medication.

"Side effects? Do you mean weight gain?" I asked the boy.

"Growing breasts. Growing breasts is one of the side effects. I just want you to know."

I hope I wasn't obvious as I looked the boy over, wondering if he was on Risperdal.

When he sensed that I needed to make my way home, Adrian held fast to my leg. Abandoning his block tower, he pleaded, "take me with you, Mom!" If only this tormented little soul knew that I wished for nothing more. My little son, who cannot project what he needs two minutes outside of this moment, is unable to make sense of what has happened to him, and certainly cannot understand that the "staff" needs him to demonstrate certain behaviors before he can come back to us.

"Adrian! Your mom is leaving!" puffed Helen, a stately and stern sixty-ish-year-old woman who forced others to earn her smiles. She called a nurse colleague to peel Adrian from me, and I could hear his anguished cries down the hallway, past windowless walls bearing what must have been forced watercolor paintings by inpatient artists. I saved my own sobs for the drive back to Elmhurst. I expect that I, too, would be somewhat hardened and abrupt if I dealt with young patients who, on an hourly basis, kicked hard at my desk and called me an "idiot" and a "dumb ass."

I am learning more on this journey of parenting than I ever expected to learn. Honestly, I really don't want to learn all this stuff. I don't want to know the side effects of Risperdal. I don't want to have a reason to need to know them. I don't want others to treat my sweet boy with any less dignity than he deserves. The grip of mental illness is not selective. This child is only trying to make sense of his world and his emotional kaleidoscope. I want him to eat lemon shortbread, I want him to be able to walk across the train tracks without being gripped by fear, and I want him to enjoy the Christmas lights with the rest of us. I want him to know that he is a treasure and a great blessing, every single day.

God, I miss him.

Fear of Falling

(May 18, 2015)

If we didn't let them climb the tree, they never would.

Last night, I sat with my love of twenty-five years (tomorrow!) as we watched two of our boys blast one another with the garden hose. We have called the contractor to repair the sidewalk, but at this moment in time, I was glad he had not yet come. I was glad there were puddles, and I was glad my boys were soaking up the mud. Dan had stolen my thoughts as he wondered aloud if it might be their last night together.

Earlier in the weekend, Dan had crafted three steps and fastened them to the best climbing tree in the yard; now even the tiny ones could be that much closer to the sky. Adrian, upon returning from his three-minute birding adventure in his new hideout, announced that he had spotted one bird. He then turned over Grandma Ihm's vintage binoculars and began plotting his next scheme. He had, though, been high up in the tree for the first time.

In a parade of stroller and bicycles, we filled more of our Saturday with a trip to the dollar store for ice cream treats. It had been a full day, and it had been as pleasant a weekend as we have had in a long time.

Of course, there is always redirection, and a rare day goes by without a physical struggle that results in a hold. I had felt my fingernails meet his smooth, pink flesh. I hoped I didn't scratch him as I struggled to reason with this beautiful, fiercely unsettled seven-year-old. I am not as strong as I used to be. And I don't know why your game isn't loading, sweet boy. I'm so sorry.

I'm sorry for everything. I am sorry for the railroad tracks, the thunder, the bees, the wind, and for everything that invades your head and stirs your fears.

We are strong, through our weaknesses. We have no choice.

Adrian was calm and complacent during this morning's routine. After finishing his "sixteen" pieces of cinnamon toast, he asked if Robin would mind if he ate his leftover crusts. I offered to make him another piece, and he assured me that this would be a good idea, since Robin's crusts were probably full of drool. My boy, I will make you a million pieces of cinnamon toast. As we watch for the bus, I am reminded of a year ago where each morning was its own circus act. My heart would beat a mile a minute as I struggled to nearly drag him to the bus each and every morning.

Now, he knows. The morning fights are rare; he watches for the bus, and he has resigned himself to the fact that he goes to school each morning. Looking back from my calm morning today, I can certainly see that my boy has grown.

I know, and I am on high guard. I know that I was told on Friday that the hill is very steep, and that there is no traction. I wait for the call, because I have been told that the time will be soon, that intervention seems, once again, inevitable. We don't want to go back. We have come so far.

We don't want to go back where he is not understood, where nobody sits with him as he falls asleep, and where he is presented with trays of brown things with gravy. We don't want to go to a place where the outcome will be no different than the last time.

Then the moments come, and there is nothing we can do. There is nothing anyone can do. We will be strong for him, and for them, because they are all we have.

My hip is bothering me a little bit these days, and I know, it's a function of overuse. Of course. But I am sure I could still climb that tree, at least now that there are a few steps to help me up. If I were to climb the tree, though I may fall, I would also see far and wide, and long into the future.

I am sure that I would see him, and I am sure that he would be okay. He would be smiling, walking across the railroad tracks in a thunderstorm, and as soon as he came through the back door, I would make him as much cinnamon toast as he wanted.

The Solo

(June 9, 2015)

She was hoping to find time to walk to the dollar store for a replacement pair of fake eyelashes, as her current ones were getting a bit "gooey." She had worn them to play practice, to the gaming store, to the neighborhood park, and even to the horse barn for her riding lessons. Now that the layers of glue were nearly as thick as the lashes themselves, it was time to invest in a new pair, which would be the perfect finishing touch for her dance recital, for her first solo. She had told me days earlier that she was ready to quit dance lessons.

The door opened and we filed in, making our way to the metal folding chairs neatly lined in three rows. I preferred to sit toward the back, in the last row, up on the riser and near the door. It was stifling in the upstairs studio, but through the open balcony door, a welcome spring breeze caught the new garden blooms and diluted the aroma of worn pointe shoes and cheap perfume. I had come here to watch dozens of dance recitals over the last decade, and as the lights dimmed, I was keenly aware that this might be my daughter's last recital.

She had a few minutes of fame, and she was strong and beautiful. I do not remember the music, but the song will play on in my head. She is not a little girl anymore. And I did not even notice her eyelashes.

The bat bag was hanging in the farthest corner of the basement, on the sturdy hook where it had been for the last three years, and where it was nearly forgotten, until the dawn of Robin's first t-ball practice. I couldn't remember if the youngest players needed equipment, but I am always more comfortable when I am prepared. I was not ready, though, for what I found in the bag. That last game had given me reason to believe that I would be watching my boy on the mound well into his high school years. Little did I know that music, theater, and the social obligations of high school would be more important to Kevin than my beloved game. They would make him happier, as happy as playing baseball once did. And little did I know that when the last out had been recorded and he zipped the bat bag, my lefty pitcher was closing this era of his childhood.

The dust rose to greet me as I dug through the enormous bag, which would be a bit overpowering for our tiny Robin. There they were, all lefties: the catcher's mitt, the first-baseman's glove, and the fielder's glove, all from days beyond, all beckoning to once again be part of summer's game. The smell of leather was the same, and I thought of Kevin as he skipped off the mound with his constant presence of joy, no matter if he had struck out the side or given up five runs. His last game had been a stellar performance in a game that mattered none. But really it did, because they all do. Robin, though, throws with his right hand. I took the bag but put the gloves on the shelf with the abandoned ice skates and deflated air mattresses.

I was a helper at the "chalk and bikes" station for field day at the school last week. Robin's class was the first at my station. One small boy struggled to keep up with the pedals on his sturdy steel tricycle. He pulled up next to me, planted his feet on the ground below, and peered upward. Every word came guarded, with a mountain of effort. "I like…I think…I…you look…pretty." His smile was enough to make me know that he was more than just a day brightener. He, who had likely overcome more challenges and obstacles in his first four years of life than I had in my nearly half century, had come to deliver a message. I knew my tears were lined up, waiting to fall. There could be no crying for this preschool helper mom, though I would have certainly been met with a compassionate audience. I looked down at my pink shirt, at the spatter of bleach stains that had begun to wear into holes. The shorts I wore were my favorites, secondhand and frayed. I knew that even just a few years from now, my little friend would not tell me what he had said that day. The years would mark him, and they would take away the breathtaking beauty of his innocence that, on that day, for me, had been akin to a delivery of fresh roses.

My children are growing up. Some are no longer children at all. Some I have held as infants, while others came to me at a much older age. Still I am their mama, and they will always be my children. I watched James drive off to the city yesterday afternoon, after one last family trip to the frozen custard stand. He had late word of an internship and, though he knows not where he will live or what his position will be, he is brave and bold, and ready to open what the world has given. My new son Austin, my adult son, will soon leave us to travel across the ocean to follow his true calling. Their childhood games, their artistic passions, their youthful spirits, and even the challenges that they have faced, have all given meaning to who they are becoming as men and women. If my daughter has danced her last dance, and if my boy has pitched his last fastball, that must mean that they are ready, even if I am not, for what awaits.

I will pine for the innocent child that you once were, but I will celebrate who you have become, all on your own. And when your journey brings you back home to me, I will be there, ready to embrace all that is you, and fake eyelashes included.

Into the Darkness: Factory Sealed

(June 22, 2015)

It was her birthday. There wasn't going to be a party, because she wouldn't be able to come.

I begged her to sleep, imagining that she was on my lap in the white wicker chair that had rocked her brothers before. We would be reading "Little Fur Family", my favorite Margaret Wise Brown book, a book which has offered a different sort of comfort with each child that I have held and rocked.

Don't be afraid. Don't be scared. I'm here with you. But what if I'm scared, too?

I saw a middle-aged woman walking into a downtown restaurant just the other day. I don't remember which restaurant it was, but my memory of the woman is bright as the January snow on a sunny morning. Her name is Donna, and I first met her when I was in college. My friend and I were helping at a church that provided shelter for people in the community that had no place to sleep at night. We had to arrive sharply at the start of our shifts, as the doors were locked once everyone was accounted for, and no one could come or go until seven in the morning, at which time all the "guests" were sent forth into the shadows of the community until evening fell once again.

"Maybe you could do something with my hair." I turned to find the source of the meek voice, and I was face-to-face with a girl, a woman, who looked to be about half a decade past my starry-eyed nineteen years. She was Donna, and she had a sweetness and youthfulness about her that matched the lisp in her words. There was something, though, behind the wonder of her wide eyes, that led me to believe that her childhood had been met with circumstances which had tried to take some of that innocence away. As I French braided Donna's hair, I must have secretly wondered how she had come to be here, how she had come to be a "guest" at the shelter.

"I'm hungry for brownies!" The booming voice came from John, whose commanding presence and permanent scowl evoked fear from a place deep inside of me. "I want brownies," he again caused my spine to stiffen. I peered toward my friend, and the collective decision was made. John was going to get brownies, because we were afraid of what would happen to us if we didn't come through. There were no eggs, but the "person in charge," perhaps also aware of the potential wrath of John, unlocked the basement door so we could venture into the darkness to buy a dozen eggs from the convenience store, which was just up the road. John, expressionless, devoured brownie after brownie as we looked on with a combination of terror and relief.

There is a man that walks to a rhythm. He takes some steps, spins to face the opposite direction on the sidewalk, takes some more steps, then spins to his original spot and continues along. I wonder where he is going; I wonder if he knows. He looks somehow familiar, like someone I may have known many years ago. I may wonder, but there really are no answers.

We have known all along. The darkness has gotten darker, and nobody can find the lights. Our girl needs more than we have to give. Sweet sixteen, and she is not home. She can't be home. It wasn't her; she wasn't there.

I am so, so sorry.

I can hear those words again, and I think of my tiny book which is covered in fake fur. The words, even the thought of those words, still my soul.

"You can bring me snacks to eat when you visit, but they have to be factory sealed. Nothing homemade." Her request was somewhere between Donna's braids and John's brownies on the continuum of insistence. Happy Birthday, indeed.

When she was very small, I took my baby girl to Oakbrook Mall. She was carrying on, and she did not need anything in particular (at least not anything that I could provide). "Take that baby home and put her to bed!" The words of a stranger bit through my being as tears welled in my eyes. I wanted to tell this person that my little girl doesn't sleep, that she is never settled, and that I just thought we both needed a little time walking in the fresh air where the tulips were in full, perfect bloom. I stayed silent. I should have said what my friend had the courage to say when his young family was met with jeering and condescending stares from fellow restaurant patrons.

"You have no idea what they have been through."

I have no idea what she, the girl that I have held and rocked, has been through. And I will never, ever know.

When I saw Donna the other day, nearly thirty years from our last meeting, she was with another woman. It seemed that this woman was her friend, and they both looked happy, smiling and engaged in conversation as they entered the restaurant.

Braids, brownies, even a factory-sealed birthday cake for your sixteenth birthday...if it's what you want, if it's what will make you happy in this moment, then that is my wish for you, that we can overcome the fear.

I hope you get your wish, and I hope that one day, every day, you will be happy.

Bigger Than Me
(November 8, 2015)

We used to plan our outings around his fears. When Adrian was a very small boy, I could push the stroller as fast as my feet could carry us. We may have been nearly across the railroad tracks before he knew. As he grew older and his supernatural power of directionality kicked in full force, he was more keenly aware of the shadows where his fears were held captive. We would go only to the parks on our side of the train tracks, and we would save our trips downtown to the candy store for times when someone could be home to look after our boy.

The county home hosts a trick-or-treating event for children of the community on the evening before Halloween. We decided to take our children this year in hopes that we could soften their desire to spend hours on what was expected to be a blustery, rainy Saturday, on parade in pursuit of Laffy Taffy and candy corn. Our wide-eyed little ones were uncharacteristically quiet as they walked through the halls of the facility, extending their plastic pumpkins to yesterday's princesses, clowns, and witches who offered shaky fists full of Skittles, M & M's, and Smarties. I was told by more than one resident that my baby was too little for candy.

I am fearful of growing old.

We had been wondering the same thing as our eyes met over our soy lattes: how long have we been meeting like this? We deduced through memories of Christmas lists of years past that it must have been about fifteen years of the nearly three-decade span of our friendship. Yesterday, my college friend, Kate, and I had our annual ritual of meeting halfway between DeKalb and Madison on the first Saturday after Halloween. Our intentions of crossing off the holiday wish lists have, over the years, mixed gracefully with our yearly reflections of children, work, and dark chocolate. I leave home (with just a bit of guilt) to embark upon a day that truly feeds my soul. And we eat a lot, too. I don't want the day to end. As I drove home yesterday, I wished that we had taken a picture together. It has been a couple of decades since we have done that. I think, too, that when we meet next time, we will both have passed the half-century mark. We just never know what the year will bring.

Straight across the cornfields between Twombly Road and Lincoln Highway, looking from behind the Peter Rabbit crib sheet that serves as a makeshift curtain in my bedroom, I can see Mary's farm. Of course, she doesn't live there anymore, but I think of her each day as I look out my window. For all intents and purposes, Mary was my daughter's counselor. She was, though, much more than that. I would look forward to our trips to her office, where I would breathe in the peace of her stone fountain, eat with abandon from her candy dishes (always stacked to the heavens with the best types of chocolate), and fancy myself having coffee with her on a lazy Saturday. We wanted to buy her farm, and we tried hard to do just that. Now, looking over the aftermath of a Midwest harvest from my window to hers, I am better able to see the big picture.

I used to fall asleep with the television on. Some nights, I go to bed earlier than Dan while he works on his music at the edge of the bed. When we lived adjacent to campus, I was secretly comforted by the din of college students playing music and hosting bonfires even into the early morning hours. The best part of baseball season is when the Cubs play on the west coast, and I can listen to the late night games on the radio as I drift off. I just don't want the days to end.

Endings are hard. Though I wish the day could continue, I do try to remind myself of the promise that tomorrow holds.

Adrian rushed from his bus one day last week, brimming with excitement as he burst through the front door. With a new light in his eyes, he announced that he had walked across the railroad tracks with his class. Twice. And it was no big deal.

Next year, I will be sure to take that picture with Kate.

Mighty

(November 30, 2015)

"You're not my parents."

Though we may never be able to fill her up, we won't stop trying. If we were to surrender the fight, the hope would be lost. It would be gone forever. The door would slam once again, as it always has in the past, and here the story would end.

Yes, we signed up for this. We, as foster parents, have signed up for the grief, the pain, the verbal pillaging, even the remnants of trauma of past years. We signed on the dotted line, and often I think it is a good thing that we never really know what the future will hold for fear that this awareness would hold us back from answering that call.

You could feel the anger permeate the air as if it was a physical substance, pushing into the path of those fools who stood in the way and flailing through the night air in a course of bitterness.

The strength of this anger could not be contained by two adults who became weak in the wake of fury late on that Saturday night.

"You don't love me."

How I wish I could tell you what love is, how it is much more than the privilege of downloading games on a handheld device, how love means defining boundaries, commitment, and the tenacity to keep hanging in there when all around you the branches are breaking.

Our friend Eileen is a giver. She walks miles in support of causes that help those in need: children with brain tumors, people that have been affected by cancer, and, I am sure, many more. Sometimes I wonder what motivates Eileen, what drives her. I am sure that it must come from inside, from her spirit. Eileen just wakes up and does what is kind, pure, and good.

Every so often, several of my children will act out on the same day; I am sure they somehow know I am vulnerable. They stop mid-fight and decide, instead, to "get me." One is yelling at me, perhaps calling me, "Idiot Mom," and another is slapping my legs as hard as he can while catapulting shoes all over the mudroom. If it's a really bad day, one of the older ones will be cutting me, slashing me with her silence. If they see me cry, will they somehow feel like they have conquered the evil master?

They retreat. Sometimes, one or another comes forward with his best effort in a tiny heart, the word "Mom," and perhaps his own name. This is his peace offering, and something that now brings me to tears in a good way. He can see the hurt, and he wants to make it better. And he does.

Sometimes, though, the past hurts are so very deep. The anger from another life lived is so raw and so indefinable, that the targets become those that are standing by, trying to carve a path toward promise. There is no "sorry" here; there are definitely no hearts. Just a mighty torrent of fear, anguish, and the deepest kind of pain.

Inside, I know she is a giver, just like our Eileen. She would, and does, step up to help as she can. I have seen her light...and I have seen it flicker and try to go out, doing its best to burn those that stand in the way.

Time and again, we are reminded that this is not about us. And time and again, we must remind ourselves that we are human and that we, too, must be given the grace to grieve alongside her.

We know now, after half a dozen mental health hospitalizations among several of our children between this November and the last, when the force is bigger than us, and when we must call for help. We know now when our love just isn't enough.

We know that we signed up for this. When we answered the call, when we set another spot at the table, when we embraced, when we have been embattled, and when we have laughed and prayed together...we were not prepared, but we never could have been.

"I would rather spend the rest of my life here than go home with you guys."

And maybe, deep inside, that might seem easier than working out what this is really about. But when the urge for hot Cheetos hits, it seems like a pretty good time to offer the olive branch and to call home.

We want her to come back. We know, though, that there is plenty keeping her there that has nothing to do with us.

So we signed up to fan the flames, to try to make peace with an uncertain past, and to know that if and when there are words and understanding, our collective healing can begin.

And we would do it all over again, even many times, because when we signed up for this, we were not answering a call but a calling, a privilege to do a work bigger than we are, to do God's work.

And when she is ready, we will be waiting. We will put the lights, sirens, and fierce words behind us as we share another bag of hot Cheetos.

Wings

(December 15, 2015)

It's a true moment of joy each morning as I watch my forty-pound (fully clothed) bundle of happiness burst forth from the front door and sprint across the now snow-covered yard to meet his bus.

This is not because he is the fifth one out the door in the morning circus, but because, in that window of time as he enters the world to begin his day, he is an honest picture of happiness.

I have spent a collective week or two, at least, in my estimation, peeling preschoolers from my legs, hauling combative children to the bus, or driving away from morning drop off, haunted by the screams (of my child, certainly) that permeated the hallway along with the smell of crayons and library books.

"I don't like kindergarten," Robin announced convincingly after just a few days at his new school. "It takes too long to get back to you."

And it truly does. Eight hours is nearly an eternity for me on many days as I wait for my little son, my sun, to come home. This tiny light was surely to be our last baby, and when he would start school, I would return to my job that I walked away from when Adrian came to us as a newborn, eight years ago.

One morning last week, my sure-footed little sprite slipped on his way to the bus. He fell to the wet ground, landing on his hands and knees. I had no time to even wonder if he was okay as he popped up and skipped the rest of the way to Bus 1, smile still sparkling. The smile, though, did not keep my heart from breaking into a million pieces, nor did it keep me from worrying all day if he was cold from the wet grass. It takes so very long for him to get back to me.

When I had outpatient surgery in junior high, my mom brought me a flower bouquet. It was a yellow chrysanthemum with black pipe cleaner eyes and mouth fashioned to create a smiley face. This may have been the moment that spurned my passion for gardening; I adored that flower. Over time, the yellow loveliness began to fade to an unhealthy looking brown and, the once sweet springtime fragrance was now actually a little bit foul. The smile was indiscernible. I took my flower to the garbage.

I don't remember if it was later that night or the next morning when I could no longer bear the feelings of guilt and sadness. I pulled the wilted, spent flower, still holding fast to its green floral foam amid empty tuna cans, baseball card wrappers, and apple cores, from the garbage bin. It was given a place of honor on the shelf in my closet, where it was allowed to shrivel and drop petals in peace.

My friend's daughter left for the Navy last week. This child that she held and rocked will not be home for Christmas; perhaps not until next summer. She is brave and ready, but my friend will not be able to help her up when she falls on her way to the bus anymore. There will be things...falls, disappointments, and even pain...about which my friend may never know.

I didn't get to help my son Austin when he fell. I was not there to see him take his first step, get on the bus for his first day of kindergarten, or play his first football game. Then, I did not even know him. Last May, already an adult, he became an official member of our family. A few short months later, he flew across the ocean to pursue his longtime dream of becoming a priest.

Though I am all for finding one's wings, the bridge of transition is a hard one.

My first-born son, Jonathan, is now the same age as I was when I gave birth to him. As a preschooler, he waited at least twenty minutes alongside his little friend Jade as they held out for the engineer's cab, where you could pull the chain to sound the bell, on the train at Yorktown Mall. Just as they were ready to board, two older boys stormed past our blindsided little ones and into the choice cab. It was all I could do not to burst into tears as I felt the disappointment and defeat of our four-year-olds.

We love so hard and so deeply, it is almost as if we are part of them.

Robin was not, after all, to be our caboose. There was another little boy. There was another chance at riding in the engineer's cab, at attending little league games, and at watching a flower unfold. There was another chance to hold on to the passage of time, to feel deeply in the moment, and to rejoice in the gift of these wings, wherever they may fly.

The Call

(February 10, 2016)

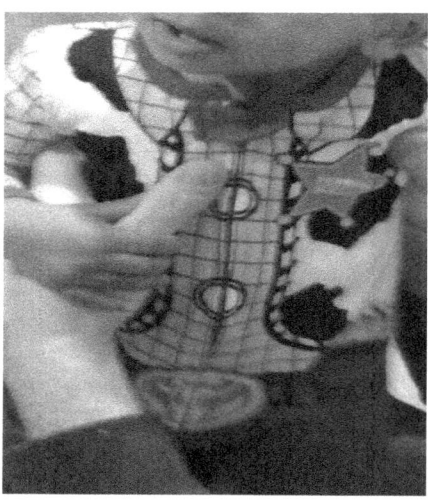

It had been three days more than a year since the day that I took this boy home. I was never good at leaving my kids; I prefer to have them with me all the time. I think that's just because I always want to know that they are okay. What if I hadn't had my spot on the hot metal bleachers in Wasco on the day James broke his ankle on his way back to first base? What if he had needed me, and I had not been there?

I needed Alice, and she was there. Her whole family was there. When you learn that your little son, who really isn't wholly, completely, only your son, since he was born to another mother, has a baby sibling that will enter the foster care system, something happens inside of you. You need your son to know that sibling, and you need to be able to raise that sibling, that baby boy, with your little son if that baby cannot be with his birth family. The very thought of what has transpired during this recent space of time, a space that hollowed me with a depth of sadness that I could not have fathomed, and then lifted me to a joy that has no barriers, sends forth a river of tears. The tears are for the grief of the mother of these little boys; for the loss to my friend and her family; for the boys who have a connection that could only have been forged by a higher power; for other siblings to these boys that they may never really know; and for our creator who certainly knows the meaning in the brokenness, and the gifts in the rebuilding.

He is so busy these days: a typical, active toddler, skilled at scaling boxes in the mudroom and at emptying library shelves in record time. I knew when I dropped him at Alice's house while I took my daughter to a couple of appointments, he would be in the most capable of hands, the hands that held and embraced him on that fateful day one year and three days ago when he needed a home.

The state has rules. The state wants the brothers to be together, but when the house is already full, the rules loom first and foremost. There are many papers to sign, many workers to look over the papers, and even more stamps to be applied to these papers. Sometimes, all of these things need to happen all over again. These are people, precious lives. But there are many rules.

I was shaking when the call came. Of course we will take the baby. I stopped at Walgreens on the way to the DCFS office to get some formula and nursery water; the other essentials were already at home from the many little ones who had come before. I had a sinking feeling that I would be leaving empty-handed that afternoon, because of the rules.

"You came for your baby!"

A familiar investigator offered the tiny bundle. I tried not to allow myself to melt as I held the sleeping angel and waited for the placement to clear, because I knew about the rules.

"I'm sorry. They can't place him with you now."

Before the tears could fall, I thought of Alice. Her young family was just recovering from a winter sickness, and I knew that she must be exhausted. But there was never the slightest hesitation. The paperwork was completed, and my son's baby brother was on his way to my friend's house.

To give fully of yourself, knowing quite well that this act will end in deep loss, that is the ultimate gift of self that can neither be repaid nor replaced.

To appreciate and to celebrate the bond of siblings in the true spirit of child welfare, in the spirit of true friendship, is to answer a call that holds no promises, in this moment or ever.

For two long months, Alice held this baby through the night. She and her family gave him what he needed, and she loved him with her whole self, because, in that moment of time, he was her baby.

The papers were stamped and signed, and the rules were satisfied. One year and three days ago, he came home. And with this new beginning, he left the family that had truly answered the call. It was late when I arrived. Alice and her husband were quiet, though still welcoming. Their eyes bore the sadness of loss as their hearts ushered forth what was to come: their baby, my baby, but not wholly mine or theirs…was going home, to my home with his brother, at least for now.

If I hadn't been at the game that day long ago, still James's ankle would have healed. But I'm glad I was by his side through the fear. Alice did not have to answer the call. Had she not, our baby Joey would have been cared for in another home until the work was done. Our friends put their fears aside, though, in the true spirit of foster care…and friendship…and made a big difference in the lives of two boys, and two families.

"I would do it again in a heartbeat," she said. And I know she really meant that.

When my daughter's appointments were done and I had dropped her back at school, I drove through downtown, across the railroad tracks, and on to Alice's house to get my little one. I could see him through the porch window, playing alongside the little boy very near to his own age that joined Alice and her family; curiously, just short of a year ago, and just weeks after Joey had left.

There were no tears this time when I took him home. Alice reminded me that he is where he is supposed to be. And when I watch my two littlest boys roll about and chase each other until sunset, both with the same sideways sparkle in their eyes, I know that this must be true.

Through all of the stamps and paperwork, even through the loss and the grief, this is about honoring the bond of siblings. It's about putting your dreams aside in favor of something that surely must be sacred.

I am grateful to my friends, for celebrating with us, for being part of our journey, and for being able to see, even with their eyes closed, the deepest meaning.

■■■

In the beginning, I thought I would be enough. I was sure that I could be, and that I should, at least along with Dan, be able to help them through the darkest parts. Now I know, and our family knows, that sometimes the need for help is greater than what we have to offer. I have learned that such a thing is okay: the big picture does matter, but so, too, do all the little moments along the way.

There was not just one hospitalization, just as there was not just one hole in the wall or just one piece of furniture damaged during the wrath of overwhelming emotion. Almost as if I was watching the events unfold from afar, I wondered what was to come, and how we might make it to the other side. So far, we have. I have my ticket, and I have gotten on the bus.

There is no way to forget the long hours spent in the emergency room, waiting for the inevitable and, eventually, turning my small boy over to the unknown, to the strong but foreboding arms of the man that would transport him to the hospital when we had lost our fight. Adrian did gain more than twenty pounds in a few short months while taking Risperdal, which he no longer takes because it was ineffective to quell his behaviors. And, it is too early to tell if the boy with the red streak was right.

Susanne visited our farm for the first time last week. It was a good day. We cried a collective of tears as we shared visions of those early days, with Jonathan, James, Jade, and her little brother playing in the grass outside the Starry Sky while we sat on a nearby bench and drank iced lattes. This visit, though we did not sit for long at all, was every much as soul satisfying as before.

We now have many trees at the farm, and there is much potential to continue to climb to brighter days. Adrian still requests cinnamon toast at least once a week, though it has been a long time since he has asked for a specific number of pieces. His fears of railroad tracks and thunderstorms have subsided. He does not, though, tolerate moths, flies, mosquitoes, or bees, all of which are abundant during this time of year, especially in the country. I do not much like them either.

As for my ballerina, there were pleas to take classes again, and there was another recital, followed yet again by her "retirement," this time "for good." There is, though, still much dancing across her days.

My tears fall for missing them, but there is more: they fall because as my children grow older, they do not need me as much as they once did, at least not in the same way. My tears fall because I know they have wings of their own, and because I cannot keep them by my side, in the safety of the nest forever. I know that though they have been through their share of trials, they have aspirations and wishes all their own. My wish is that one day they will be met with the happiness that comes from knowing that they are deeply loved, and that their wishes, their futures, do matter.

I guess I am afraid to grow old for fear of releasing control. As I struggle with endings every day, I am comforted by holding the thought that an ending is just the beginning of a new adventure.

Austin, the oldest child in our lineup, has been home from his mission work abroad for a time this summer. The day was perfect and sunny, and we had been out running some errands. I knew he had things to do at home, but I really needed to get some compost and peat moss from the garden store. A twenty-pound toddler and two forty-pound bags of garden amendments are not easily handled, so I just thought I would ask.

"Would you mind if I ran to the garden store to pick up a couple things...and could you stay with Joey in the car?" I did not anticipate the magnitude of his response.

"Sure. Besides, I like spending time with you, Mom."

My son, you have no idea.

Later that very day, Jonathan called me from California. He is just days from a major written exam that will play quite a hand in his future. Generally inspired and confident, and certainly gifted in his knowledge base, it seems he had left a little room for self-doubt and insecurity to creep into the days leading up to this event. We talked about chickens and mindfulness, and I reminded him that it was he that taught me that a bit of anxiety can be motivational for success. Just as I couldn't keep him from missing out on the engineer's cab all those years ago, I cannot ease the burden of his work. Before ending the call, he expressed that it was good that we had talked, and that his thoughts were a bit more clear. In reality, though, I was the true benefactor of his call, of knowing, as I pulled crabgrass and wild violets from the soil at the side of the barn, some forty hours away by car from this beloved boy, this child of mine, that he was, in that moment, okay.

And some days, when I struggle to wonder where the meaning lies, I think of Alice, and of what she did for my little boys, who will one day soon be big boys. Alice's family now has two more little boys in their bustling home. Looking forward through her grief at handing the bundle that was tiny Joey to me, and knowing that it was possible that he may not even have stayed long term with my family, she knew that he most certainly was not going to stay with hers. I wonder, knowing what we now know, if the transition would have been easier. Though it likely may have been, the gifts that have come with the trust in accepting that which is beyond our control are truly magic, and truly the work of something more than we are.

THE SIGNIFICANCE OF OTHERS

"I don't know how you do it."

I don't do it, not alone, anyway. Nobody does; nobody can do what they do, truly on their own. We need people. We need people to teach us lessons, to catch us when we stumble, to make us chocolate cake with vanilla frosting, to love us without barriers, and to tell us that everything is going to be okay. Without others, there would be no reason to, well, be.

Sometimes, I didn't know just how much someone would mean to me until I looked back. Life marches on, and I am sometimes lonely even in the company of others. The importance, though, of standing alongside, of being there even when we are not sure our place, is real. I am sharing stories of what I have learned from a tiny child whose stay on this earth was short, from her family, and from the deep meaning that they have shown to me. I am sharing a story of the wisdom of a young mother, of how I have learned to love more deeply and freely by the example that she has shown. There are stories of those who have meant something to me in my childhood, and how these experiences have carried me through the present day. There is great comfort in knowing that I can turn to those who have walked alongside me, knowing that they will believe in me through uncertainty and even when I may not believe in myself.

Standing Small
(April 3, 2014)

The abandoned barn sits on a gravel drive, which curves into a well-traveled road at the edge of town. I always "almost" forget about it until it looms a stone's throw away, lonely in its befallen glory, with rotting wood of perfect red struggling to boast its last hints of dignity as it succumbs to the cruelty of relentless Northern Illinois weather. Nobody comes, day after day, year after year, to tend to its weary boards.

I felt the soul of that barn today. I thought that I sometimes feel like that lonely barn. Surrounded by the chaos that presents itself from sunrise to sunset, and sometimes even through the night, I am sometimes still alone.

Several of my friends became grandmothers this early winter. And with my vicarious celebrations (I do look forward to one day sharing this fate!) comes the stark realization that time is passing. Like the barn, I am aging. I cannot stop the wiry grays from infiltrating my dishwater hair.

When we took the family to visit Dan's mom two Sundays ago, she was slumped on the couch, fast asleep on the shoulder of another resident. It had been a while since we had been out to see her; there was a marked difference in her mobility. As Dan reached to assist the woman that had held him on her lap and nursed him to toddlerhood, she startled awake and let him hold her steady on her feet. Though the light of her smile pleads to tell us differently, she no longer recognizes me or my row of ducklings. She is grateful for the company, yes. Something about her, though, understands that we are her people. For that hour, she played cards with her grandchildren, ate a bite of pizza, and feigned understanding of the questions that she likely did not realize she was asking. As we left her in her chair, I glanced back to see the sun fading; her eyes reminiscent of the hallowed windows on the lonely barn.

Our child came to us in a fury of screams. The years have passed and, through many services, the door often does not open. It is held shut by something: past trauma; lack of attachment; a primal wound too deep to heal. A lonely barn, surrounded by people.

I looked back at the landscape as I drove a bit further into town. From a distance, the loneliness seemed to fade. The barn became part of a vibrant university community. I retraced my path, parked the van, and approached the barn. With just enough room to retreat safely if I were apprehended, I stared. How frightened, how alone that barn looked when I was standing beside it. The memory of a flowering vine threatened me with its sharp, up close, seasons-since-bearing-beauty barrenness.

My dear longtime friend lives just across the road from that barn. When she faces the direction of the field and looks out at the barn, I like to believe that a small bit of its loneliness goes away. When we make ourselves available to others, when we stand alongside, when we understand that we may not understand…I like to believe that that, alone, has to be enough.

Driving to the Angels

(May 8, 2014)

Adults cannot find the meaning of life; it has already been discovered by all of the children. Today, I traveled a road that I have not driven in many years. The back roads of DeKalb county have led me to some of my deepest blessings, blessings and experiences that have caused me to look deep within myself as I, too, walk an uncertain (and often tumultuous) path. My small son rode along with me this time. My fear was that if I did not make the trip today, I might be too late. The shop where I always stopped for my cranberry nut muffin has long since closed. There was the elusive stop sign that woke me from one last reverie. I knew we were nearly there as we came to the turn in the road; this was where I had pulled aside in a rainstorm, having been caught on my way to the car in a spontaneous downpour. Her mama, though, had a towel waiting for me as I arrived at the farmhouse, which always smelled of lavender. Her mama was one of my deepest sources of comfort even in the early days, when I was sent by the State to support her. In the early days, when hope was fresh and there were still so many avenues which might lead to…an answer of some sort, or at least more hope. In the early days, when there wasn't reason to entertain thoughts of years down the road, because we didn't know. Perhaps we didn't want to know. In those early days, I saw in that family the truest, most raw sense of living life as it was given. Yes, there was hope, but there was also concern, and, above all, there was a love so deep, I know I fell in.

And so today, when there is not much time left at all, I held her hand for what might possibly be one last time. On my knees at the strength and valor of this extraordinary family, I have been given the gift of knowing a true angel. We didn't stay long. My son, at four, knew. "It's okay, Mama. Now she is going to be with God." I am pretty sure I hadn't said a word.

"Do you want my George?" I am not sure if I nodded or reached for a tissue, but he offered up his little blue elephant. He shared with me what comforted him, and in that moment, my grief was softened by the animal on my shoulder, and by the true love of a tiny boy.

Please know, the sweetest of angels, what a vastly more beautiful place our world is because of the years that you have been here, and because of the meaning that you have given us, and because of the lessons that you will continue to teach as you stretch your wings to those who have been blessed to know you.

Glad That's Not My Kid... Oh, Wait...It Is!

(June 29, 2014)

I have a new friend. Well, relatively new, in the scope of things. Alice, a fellow foster mom, has a load of kids, just like me, and it seems we are connected on enough levels that there is no explanation necessary during a long pause. I am pretty sure, though, that there are not many long pauses, if any at all. I would wipe the snotty nose of any of her children, and I am guessing she would do the same for mine, even the teenagers.

Spontaneous meet-ups are the best. Arranged play dates are often disastrous, and "bookstore gatherings" are something of the distant past. It's best to meet at a park, and to call such a meeting when little people are already strapped in strollers and the bike riders are ready to roll. It's day by day, and one moment before the next. I am peaceful and comfortable sitting (for a few seconds, maybe) on the park bench with Alice. In a foggy and distant way, I feel like I am at the Starry Sky with my precious Elmhurst mama friends, where we did sit for hours, and our babies stayed within a six-foot radius and smiled the whole time while we drank vanilla lattes and ate lemon shortbread.

We were probably talking about someone smashing something valuable when I looked up and noticed a tiny child dangling by the knees from a considerably high playground perch. Distracted enough from the conversation by this miniature acrobat, I remember thinking that I was glad this was not my kid engaged in such an unsettling and dangerous maneuver. But it was, indeed, at second glance, my child. My thirty-pound four-year-old wonder was flaunting circus skills that were, for the first time, revealed to me. And he was okay.

A couple of decades ago, terror would have caused me to spring to the rescue. Now, my knees are crunchy, and I no longer "spring." I think I am, out of necessity and with Alice's help when I need it, learning, instead, to breathe. We had a family trip last week; we spent time at Lake Michigan with all of our children to open the gates of summer. Looking back, it was a good time. As we were still unloading the car and sorting through our sandy beach bag, our foster daughter was gathering her belongings, ready to move on to a new home. She couldn't say precisely why, but we all felt the many reasons through the angst and emotion. A little time has passed, and though it is not easier to understand, we learn to take ourselves out of the equation. We learn to accept that the burdens that have come before, and the jaw-dropping surprises, good and bad, are far removed from our control. These days are not what I may have written, but they are mine and ours, and there is so much good.

We sat in the "cry room" at church when Jonathan was a toddler, in case he coughed or made a peep of some sort. Once another mom (three children, all eating pretzels) offered a snack to Jonathan. I politely declined, because my child was not going to eat junk food during church. Now, I am pretty sure I would let them eat the pretzel crumbs that they found on the floor of the "cry room." But we wouldn't likely be sitting in the "cry room." My younger set might be hanging on various monuments around the church, and I can only hope that I would notice.

Alice was a newborn baby when I was in high school. From her, though, I have learned much. There are some things that are out of our control, but when we confront and embrace the fears that we face, we might grow and learn to love more freely and deeply. To cherish others for who they truly are, and to celebrate and learn from each little circus performer: this will remain my task. And I have lots of jobs to do.

The Music in my Head

(November 20, 2014)

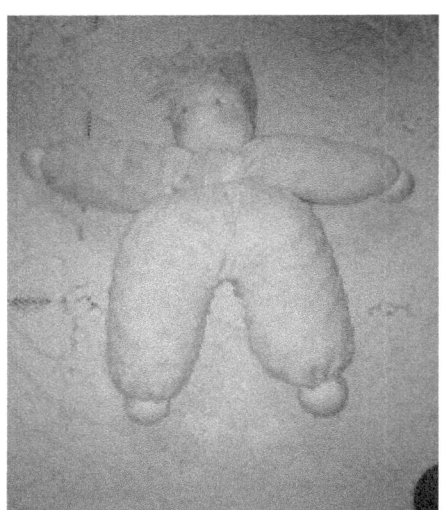

I don't remember if she listened to music, but surely she must have.

Carrie may not have seen herself as such, but she was the subject of my deep admiration…even envy… throughout our hood. With her china doll features, porcelain skin, wistful brown eyes, and glorious dark hair that curled softly over her shoulders, she had a sweet pink mystique about her. I loved the anticipation of walking through the "breezeway," into the kitchen of that house in Missouri, and, after a fleeting glance at the parakeets (I don't remember, but I am sure that they had names) whose cage was parked atop the chest freezer, I would enter Carrie's room, and it smelled like roses. When she was not at home, I could sit on her bed, which I found quite special and fancy, and stare at the shelves that held a vast collection of dolls of all sorts. I am pretty sure this was some form of therapy for me, as it filled my nine-year-old soul. I loved pink, I loved lace, and I loved dolls, but somehow it seemed that these things had been claimed first by Carrie, and that my interest in such things was secondary to my love for my cousin, who had no idea how much I cherished her. I told others that my favorite color was purple, because I didn't want to claim what truly belonged to another. Carrie was also a dancer, something which, though I may have aspired to be, was far beyond the realm of my capability. And I knew it, because someone once told me so. And it was definitely not Carrie, who would not have cared if I sat on her bed when she was not in her room.

"Are you still listening to that same thing?"

I was home from college on my semester break, drying my hair in my bedroom, where UB40 was blaring loudly enough to make everyone aware that I was still listening to the same thing. She had also visited the summer before I left for school, and I must have been playing the same songs.

When Chae Young arrived from Korea, Carrie, who lived with her young family outside of St. Louis in a house with plush pink carpeting, sent a tiny pink ballerina suit, complete with silk rosebuds and puffy tulle. I knew that she wanted me to know that it was okay to embrace the fanciness, the sweetness, and the balletic sparkle which was now within my grasp. Chae Young never did like dolls, but that did not stop me from initiating a small collection. Because you never know who will need to look at them; you never know who will find comfort just in knowing that they are there.

I am not sure when my obsessive tendencies began, but they continue to this day. When a song strikes a chord within me, I need to hear it, and I need to hear it a lot. I once recorded an instrumental song called "Georgetown" from a Brat Pack movie, over and again (which was not an easy feat, or a streamlined one in the days of record players and cassette tapes) until there was no more room on the tape. I would just listen and listen, and I don't think I wore headphones. These days, it is much easier to hit "repeat" on my music player until I grow weary of hearing the song. I think this habit of mine drove Dan crazy when we first met; though there was great crossover in our musical tastes, I don't think he cared to hear any song over and again for several days running. And probably he still doesn't, but he tolerates me on plenty of levels. In my despondent October days at the end of another Cubs season a few years back, I found great peace, if not healing, in Eddie Vedder's "All the Way." I listened for a string of days, until my attention and emotions turned elsewhere, and the playlist, as the time, evolved.

I think this is kind of what happens when you have autism. You need something, because it helps you. You need it over and over, because it calms you, and because it makes you feel alright (that is an Everything but the Girl song, too, by the way). So when Adrian knows the way that he needs to line up his cars, and just exactly how the cardboard has to stand, and how many pieces of wooden train tracks must be on which side of the display, and that there have to be some lentils and rice on the tracks (to look like the stones at the station), he is going to struggle if he can't, or someone else can't, make that happen. He is really going to struggle, even make loud noises or become aggressive, if we can't make it just right. The challenge is in knowing what you need, and in communicating that to those who desperately want to help you. And the greater challenge is in knowing what you need, when really you don't.

People have asked what they can do to help. And I really, really don't know. I should know. I should know how to help my little boy, but I don't. What I do know is that all of the faith, prayers, gestures, thoughts, and positive karma have great meaning. I am on my knees; grateful for all that surrounds me. When I look at the vintage cookie jar, stuffed with the goodness of Grandpa cookies (quickly devoured) that was presented by my sweet friend; when I open the brown box that contained a book that meant a great deal to the giver and just might offer some comfort during these tumultuous and trying days; when I think of how we stuffed our bellies with the taco dinner that arrived from another; when I received the sweet message of helpfulness and hope that came from another; and when I consider that people who are so very busy with their own happenings can still make time to keep my smallest boy so that I can go to the hospital to visit Adrian; I am reminded how deeply people care, and how blessed we are to be tended with such compassion and care.

If I can connect to a song that truly reflects something that I am feeling or experiencing, if I can just listen, maybe many times, I am going to feel better. If I can drown my senses in the beauty of (even the memory of) Carrie's bedroom, maybe I can go back to when my days were much simpler, when I didn't have "real" stuff to worry about.

But now that I do, I will try to embrace what I want, what I love, and what I need. I will hope that others can do the same. Whatever it takes to get through the journey, to stay on the path, to be open to the music of the moment, is what we need. Just sit with me, and listen to this song. Tomorrow will be here soon.

Is There Still Time?

(November 27, 2014)

The dishwasher is finishing its first load. As I pass through the kitchen to get my tea, I can't help but notice what lies in the enamel roaster pan: the turkey remains, post-carving, which has not yet made the journey to the garbage. I once had an art class in college, and our assignment over the Thanksgiving holiday had been to sketch the turkey carcass. I stared at the bones and leftover meat, and blended my way to a finished assignment with my charcoal and kneaded eraser. And I never gave a thought to that turkey again, until tonight.

Adrian had turkey, complete with mashed potatoes and gravy and some other indeterminable fixings, on his dinner tray when I visited him at the hospital early last week. I watched him take one bite of everything, which is remarkable in itself, before spitting each mouthful back onto his tray. Pretty soon he pushed his plate aside, stood up, and asked if I was ready to play Jenga (for about the sixteenth time). He really hadn't eaten anything at all.

This morning, when he came downstairs, he reminded me that it was Thanksgiving. And I was keenly aware. He asked if he could have Apple Jacks AND waffles for breakfast; I obliged. I cannot dig deeply enough in my soul to find understanding for how this little boy must have felt, day after day, meal tray after meal tray. He tried. He took a bite of everything. Why was he away from the people that so deeply loved and cared for him? How did we make it through those days? Here we are now, in this moment, and those days are behind us. We may not remember, but we will never actually forget.

My anxiety kicked in when I found out that the music show I had been waiting for since the beginning of time was the evening before a really important test. I was going to see 10,000 Maniacs for the first time, and Tracy Chapman was the opening act. This was as close as I could possibly get to heaven on earth as a college student, and I had the burden of an exam to study for. At the Ellington Ballroom, we were close enough to the stage to be able to nearly touch our heroes; how I wished the show would never end. The performances seemed ethereal to me, and I was filled up enough, inspired, to try to hold on to something intangible, something that I knew I needed, and that I would try my best to keep. Something to help me through the next several hours, at least, because the magic was done, and it was time to work on statistics (or whatever the class was). As I opened my notebook, I remember noticing how all of the furniture at my friend's apartment was lined up along the walls, and there was nothing in the middle of the room. Nothing, that is, except what had been there before.

When I was a little girl, my ears stuck out pretty far from my head. When I was in junior high, for some reasons that are not exactly clear to me, perhaps medical in nature, I had two surgeries to "fix" my ears. Sometimes, I think I miss my old ears. I am in touch with only a handful of people that knew me as a young child, and perhaps these old friends remember my ears as they used to be. Nobody else even knows I had different ears. But I did.

I first noticed some light patches on Robin's skin several months ago. Not long ago, he asked me why he had dots on his face. They were a bit bigger now, and I wondered if I should be concerned. After a little research and at the advice of his pediatrician,

I made an appointment to take him to a dermatologist. On the morning of the appointment, I told him that we were going to talk to the doctor about the dots.

"Why?" he questioned. "They are just part of me."

I was struck by the profound wisdom of my five-year-old. Indeed they are part of him, and when they fade in time, as they will, they still will have been there. In what will seem like the blink of an eye, they will be a memory, but they will be part of who he has been, and who he is.

My beautiful friend, Anna, is among the bravest people that I have ever met. I don't think, though, that she would identify herself as such. She lost her beloved son to leukemia, just as he was about to enter the prime of his life. He mattered, and he matters so much. His memory continues to inspire, through his family and his legacy, though he is no longer of this earth.

When my thoughts are so big I can hardly bear them, nor do justice in writing them, I can let them go, because I know they will come back to me when I am most ready. In this tiny moment, I can embrace what I can hold, and I can let the rest up to something much bigger.

When my across-the-fence neighbor called me to his side of the yard and wondered if I would like a few organic zucchini, he had no idea that I had plans to make ratatouille that evening, and the only ingredient I did not have on hand was zucchini. I hope he knew how grateful I was.

The kids were still pretty small, and I would always walk in to pick them up from the Catholic school. There was a woman named Lucia who was nearly always knitting, and I watched her. She wore a magnificent chunky pink cardigan. I told her that I loved her sweater.

"Thanks," she told me in a quiet voice. "I made it."

Some years later, Lucia's son showed up at my door with a white bag. Inside the bag was the pink cardigan.

"My mom wants you to have this."

I am grateful for my pink cardigan, neighbors bearing vegetables, Apple Jacks and waffles, my brave and inspirational friends and family, our Thanksgiving feasts, paths to understanding and healing, and each moment, though perhaps fleeting, in this beautiful life which is worthy of its own little celebration, even if it seems nobody else will remember.

Do You Think This Cake is Done?

(February 22, 2015)

It was the brightest cherry pink, and certainly richer than the kind of strawberry butter that melts into a fresh-out-of-the oven oatmeal muffin. I saw it on a resale site that I had been perusing (for maybe the second time ever) as I lay on Robin's bed, waiting for the ebb and flow of rhythmic breaths to tell me that my busy little one was finally at rest for the night or, more likely, for the next few hours. I thought of the chair, and how I really had nowhere to put such a thing; a find such as this definitely needed a spot of honor. I messaged the owner. I stopped to see the chair. I thought about it. I didn't know if I should commit. A couple days later, I went to collect it. Greeting me at the open door was a youngish man. He appeared to be wearing black dress clothing under his red velvet robe which was tied quite tightly around his slim waist. "The chair?" he queried as I turned to see a darling boy, perhaps three years old, clad in only a t-shirt and sitting with his bare bottom planted on my precious chair. The mother scooped up the boy; I handed her a fifty-dollar bill. The man offered, robe and all, to help me to the car. Pleased that I had gone through with my purchase, I thanked the curious fellow and waved as I drove away, trying not to process the unsettling details.

It's hard to know if I am doing the right thing in a given moment. It's hard to feel secure in my decisions. I have always been like this. So many times I have called my mom (who lives a thousand miles away) to ask her if she thinks the cake I am making is done, or if my pot roast has cooked long enough, or if the sour cream is still good. How would she know? She lives across the country, but I still turn to her for the comfort I need to know that everything is going to be alright. I will go back in the house, once we are all packed in the car and ready to go, to be absolutely certain that the stove has been turned off. Just to be sure. Because once the move is made, there is no going back to where we were before.

I am aware that not everyone will like the chair. Some might even find it very unappealing. I might tell those people about the boy.

I need my wise friend Jenny so much more than she even knows. The tiny little details, the ones that are made by others in their dreams, weigh on my mind late at night and steal away my sleep. I ask what she thinks, and she just assures me that what I am doing is okay, that it is all going to unfold. Just like my mom, she sends comfort in the quiet hours when the shadows are restless. She helps me know that I am doing the right thing, not because she has the answer, but because she knows me, and she knows I need to hear that she will support me in this craziness. And she does. We all need those people. We need people to believe in us.

Jenny will love the chair.

It's hard to decide where to go for dinner when we have a night out...Thai Palace? College Tap? Sombrero's? When the caseworker from the State of Illinois calls to ask if we would consider taking the baby sibling of our little son, that decision came easily, without a doubt, to me, at least. That was God, bigger than life, who, on occasion, makes His call quite clear. I wonder why I can be so tentative with the little decisions (red curry or green curry?) yet unwavering with those of the life-altering variety. I think it's because those are not up to me.

There was nowhere to put the chair; not yet. So it sat for a couple days, in the middle of the kitchen, soaking up the presence of our comings and goings, releasing the aura of the red robe/naked bottom family. In a few days' time, the chair was a glowing presence and a companion to our Peace lily, in a corner by the bookshelf in the living room. Nobody really knows about the past life of this chair; nobody knows how many times the little boy parked himself, without underwear, on this little pink piece of heaven.

It is not really like this with people, at least I don't think so. We have had many children come through our doors with stories much more intense and unbelievable; little bits and pieces, good, bad, unsettling, and likely including more than red velvet robes and the absence of underwear. They can't forget. We can't let them forget, lest they lose part of their true selves. I still have my "kitty pillow." Nothing about it has resembled a kitty for at least four decades. It is tucked away in the corner of my closet and, every so often when I dig for one sweater or another, I am reminded of the tornado, of the scary noises outside the camper, or of falling asleep on long car rides, and of how I was comforted by my (once bright pink) kitty pillow. And I am grateful, as I approach middle age, that I have my mom, and that I have jewels of friends like Jenny. They will sit with me on my pink chair, and they will help me test my cake. They will offer me the strength to know that what I am doing is okay. They know what has come before, but still they are there when I need them. I think that may be because right now, this moment, is what matters the most.

And I am so happy that I decided to get the chair.

Courage, Chickens, and the Blessings of Lifetime Friends

(July 19, 2015)

A place in the country…a few acres…maybe some chickens…somewhere for the children to run away their idle hours…peace and beauty to fill our souls as we grow old.

It's not even a dream anymore.

We are closing on our farmette this Friday. I think it is going to happen. I think this is what is supposed to happen, what has been our destiny all along.

I have been thinking of wildflowers.

To say that it has been a roundabout path is a bit of an understatement. Dan grew up in the country, in the beautifully sleepy town of Galena. In the early days of our love, he would take me to visit his mom, and we would sit high on a hill as night fell. Together, we could admire the peace and beauty of the expanses of countryside and the magnificent reflections of the evening lights on the river. I believe that yearning was stuck in his soul, and over our quarter-century together, there it must have remained, and it began to grow within me.

We can make daisy chains for the special days.

Two days ago, I drove past Crate and Barrel on the way home from taking Adrian to the autism doctor, and it reminded me of a day half a lifetime ago, when I was 24, just pregnant with Jonathan. When I met Dan, he had a band of friends that he lived with (or nearby) in the city: there were six or so that were always together, and a few others that would come and go. Some of these people had been friends from his childhood; they had shared a playpen, performed alongside one another in the school play, and left the small town safety of Galena together at high school graduation to venture forth to explore what life had to offer.

I was the outsider, an extra, a seventh or eighth wheel. In a short while, though, I was one of the tribe, and probably not just because of our shared love of vintage clothing and eclectic music. These people, Dan's people, have been there to carry me through when I had no idea I even needed their help.

We were shopping in Chicago that day, probably for Christmas. I remember feeling a little shaky, in my condition, so they found a bakery where I ate more than my share of fancy Italian cookies with bright sprinkles, buttery chocolate, and red raspberry jam filling. I also had a carton of milk for the little life inside. My days, then, already seemed rich and full.

We love our 1924 bungalow. Here I have lived as long as I have lived anywhere in my lifetime. We have made this our home: we have painted our walls, hosted parties, planted every square inch of the gardens, and raised children here. This house on South Third Street has been home to 23 children in ten years. That is a lot of fingerprints, and that is a lot of collective courage housed in the tiniest of beings...the type of courage that no one should expect to need, ever. We have done our best to love, care for, and support these children, big and small, for however long they have been part of our families. Though we have tried valiantly to tend to their needs, we often didn't even...couldn't even know what those needs were. And that's why I am so grateful for the blessings of true friends who are there to carry us along, to offer us a hand, as we try to walk along an often broken path, a path that may lead to nowhere at all.

"We can just sit for a time if we are not sure where we are going."

Maybe it's good not to know what tomorrow will bring. When the opportunity came and the pieces began falling into place, we visited the farmette. Every direction, every way we looked, there was that expanse of peace and solitude. I could almost feel Dan's heart skip a beat. We knew we would be home. It didn't matter that the hustle, the noise, and the busyness of the university was just two miles away. Here, in the grove of trees on Twombly Road, it was light years away, and that was what mattered.

Right now, here, this moment. That is what we have. Looking out at those stars in Galena was enough.

After a good cry on this Sunday morning, I understand more than ever that through the love, through the loss, through the transitions, and through the grief, there are no answers. My tribe has been there for me in so many ways over the years. Just in this window of time, they have hosted one boy for a summer internship, asking for nothing in return. They have welcomed my weary grad student for an overnight on his way to a conference, and they have offered an olive branch, playing cards, and some new clothing to our girl who has pushed us…along with her personal demons…far away. No judgment, but the pure, caring hearts of the people who understood me before I understood myself.

"I may hide, but I'm sure you'll find me."

Just as my Italian cookies and carton of milk made me feel better, the thought…the promise…of a place where we can continue to heal and grow with those we love helps me to know that through the challenges, this is exactly where we are supposed to be. And we may never, ever know.

Parts of this passage inspired by 10,000 Maniacs, "Stockton Gala Days"

■■

An empty field now holds the memory of my lonely barn, so maybe that means that after all these years, it is no longer lonely. Those that traverse that intersection may not even know about the barn, and how it stood stoically for so many years past its prime, but I do. The barn had strong purpose, and it meant something to me, and to countless others, over the decades of sunrises and sunsets.

My little angel got her wings shortly after the day that my little son Robin had been at my side as I last held her soft, pale hand. She, in a way not unlike the barn, brought comfort, purpose, and peace to those across her days. She relied on others to care for her, to support her through her days, and to love her, the latter of which came easily. We, though, needed her. And still, we are lifted up by what she taught us.

We decided to put Robin's acrobat skills to good use: he has been enrolled in a class at the local gymnastics facility which bridges karate and gymnastics. Robin is free to hang on many different bars, upside down. They even teach him...and encourage him. Though I have been taught and do believe that behavior has meaning, I am sure that some meanings are elusive, at least temporarily. I am happy, at least, that I have good people by my side who are, likely, also working on finding meaning.

With a renewed and hopeful spirit, I listen to "All the Way" as my team's magic number diminishes. It's so good to have something to look forward to, and as a lifelong Cubs fan, this is kind of a new feeling. I have cherished the radio broadcasts nearly every day through the summers since I was a child. People have asked why I listen, day in and day out. I can't say precisely, but I do know that I need to, that the rhythm of the game is music to my ears, no matter the outcome. It's hard to put thoughts into words, to tell someone what you need when you don't even know. I am grateful for the times that the light is there, and together we can forge ahead to figure it out.

I don't remember how I did on my exams the day following that concert. Never will I forget, though, the exhilaration of the show, or the loneliness of missing my little boy. I saw a picture of Robin the other day; it was taken a couple years ago, during the time when the white patches were the most visible on his face. I had nearly forgotten about those spots which had caused quite a bit of concern at the time. Like my old ears, they are a faded memory. We still carry those dear to us, those that we have lost, along with us. We must. We need them, and we remember them, because they have had a hand in making us who we are.

For now, the pink chair is in our bedroom at the farm; it looks a bit out of place as it waits for "the perfect spot." Decorated by sweaters, once-worn dry-cleaned shirts, and sheet music, it patiently awaits its moment of true reverence. The threads and strings that tie my dreams are much the same as when I was a little girl. We cannot let our children forget what their lives were like before they came to us, because all of the pages matter deeply.

I am no different than anyone else. I just need someone to let me know that it is going to be okay, and that whatever I may need to get through to the other side, that, too, is okay. I understand that they may not know, but still, it's nice to hear.

We have made it to the farm. When I am confused by the path, I can look to those that have been there with me, walked along for a while. At least I will not be alone if the path leads nowhere. I was driving with Robin the other day. "Mom, I love the farm. I am going to try never to leave." It's okay, little one. You can go along your way. Just don't forget to come back.

FINDING MEANING IN THE CHAOS

It's there somewhere; we just may not always find it. Not now, anyway. My efforts to "figure it out" usually result in more questions, which, I am pretty sure, is just fine. I have written about the curiosity of others, who ask, too, questions that may be unanswerable.

Sometimes the meaning is so clear and rich, it is almost blinding. I am sharing stories of messages and experiences that I have heard which have given me great clarity during times of deep struggle.

In my quest to follow my destiny, I am left standing in wonder as the stars align, even in sadness. My friend has died, and through this story of great loss I can more clearly see that there is a far greater purpose for each of us, something more than our earthly lives.

There is a story of regret, but regret for something that was maybe best left undone, for an invitation never sent. There, too, is a story of how the death of a tiny chick has stirred something in the soul of a small boy, something that perhaps even he did not know was there. Through the moments that string our days together, we become more of who we are. These tiny moments do, indeed, have meaning, and there they will be when we are ready for them.

I Can't Talk About It
(October 2, 2014)

"Mom, what's your favorite thing to do?" This question, posed by my teenage daughter, caught me by surprise, as I couldn't recall another time when she had asked me something that was not relative to what we were having for dinner or whether she could play games on her chrome book. The answer, though, was pretty clear.

If I could choose anything to do, I would take a walk with anyone that would go with me. If this involved pushing a stroller, that would be wonderful; if I could bring an iced coffee, that would be perfect. Since we have not yet found our farmhouse and still live in town near several childcare centers, I often see children walking with their daycare teachers. Each boy, girl, and adult holds a loop on a colorful length of material reminiscent of a leash. On a given day, I fancy that I am one of those children, strolling down Third Street, wearing my shiny silver mary janes, marching in step with my peers, breathing in all that the day has to offer and not giving a thought to what might happen this evening, much less when I am grown up.

The most remarkable of my conversations, and my most profound thoughts, seem to occur when I am walking around town or on campus. On a recent outing, Robin, almost five, wondered how old my mother was. When I told him that she is seventy-four, he asked if I, too, was seventy-four. He was not interested in hearing that I was forty-eight. Instead, he wondered if I had the same hands as Grandma. I wondered if my mother and I were to put our hands together, whether anyone would be able to distinguish hers from mine.

He, like me, is trying to figure it out.

"Mom, do most people have pink heads?" I wasn't really sure how to respond to this one. I think he answered his own question by counting his siblings and parents, envisioning each head, and coming to some sort of uncertain conclusion. I would have done the same thing.

Many years ago, when the teenagers were toddlers, I loaded Kevin and Chae Young into the purple jogging stroller, side-by-side, and ventured to campus for one reason or another. We were stopped by a strikingly beautiful Indian woman who asked, quite pointedly, if "they"…the boy with a head of blond curls and the little Korean girl…were twins. I think I attempted to respond but uttered no sound.

My friend had just finished sharing a story about her little boy, who had ordered a milkshake from a restaurant and, upon its delivery, showed his gratitude to the waitress by saying something to the effect of, "thanks, fat cow"…probably with his usual sweet smile and the purest intentions. As Robin and I made our way to the van, he broke out into his usual "windmill arm" run/skip, travelling at a rapid clip several yards ahead of me. A college girl dressed in jeans and a t-shirt and sporting what looked to be a fresh Mohawk, passed me, smiled, and commented about my little boy. Robin wondered what the student said.

"She said you're cute," I said.

"You mean HE," piped Robin, in a voice that was unmistakably heard.

Some years ago, Robin and I were at the park near the school where my son Adrian now attends. Some students from the school, which serves children with autism, were at the park with their teachers. One boy approached me several times, and I was surprised to hear him speak.

"Your kid is a brown kid?"

I nodded my head.

"Whoa!" was his response as he scurried away.

Children are innocent. The awkward comments are merely observations...functions of learning about one's world. But when does the tide change? When is curiosity not okay? I don't always know if it's okay when I am forty-eight. So I guess I choose not to ask, and not to talk about it. I find myself hoping that my little ones will not put voice to their thoughts when the situation arises...and that is probably not right. When the woman asked me about my "twins," she was really just wondering. When someone asks me if "those children" are all mine, I am happy to tell them so. People are curious. And, often, awkward.

I guess there is a comfort level that I can only strive for, that I can never actually reach. It's out there, and I can feel it, but I don't know what to do with it. And that is going to have to be okay, because I am pretty sure nobody else really knows either. I think I will just continue walking with my little ones, searching for answers, and finding more questions. At least, if it's a good day, I will have my coffee.

I Just Think You're Really Beautiful

(November 11, 2014)

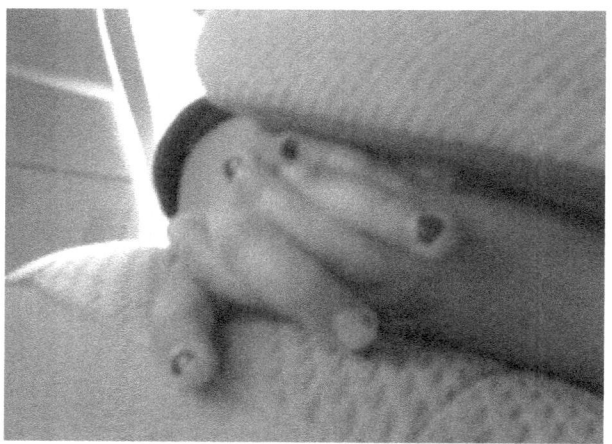

I haven't been to church in over a year. For many reasons, really, I found myself in the back row this Sunday. I knew it was going to be hard. It's often the music, maybe because of ways that music in all forms has played its way through my years with Dan. We are together because a mutual friend noticed an indie rock band poster that hung on the walls of each of our college dorm rooms. She knew that the Everything but the Girl fans should meet. Our record collections were nearly identical. Dan played his guitar for me, and sung his way to my heart. In so many ways, my blessings abound.

Sometimes I can't get the tears to stop, and once they come, they carry all the brokenness over the wall. This was happening Sunday, when words to a worship song were offered to me as obviously as if a gentle, open hand presented them directly. I knew something greater must be happening when "Ezekiel" appeared on the screen that announces, among other things, the scripture readings. That is my little boy's middle name. The little boy whose needs are so very big.

It has never been easy for me to play board games. I find it hard to pay attention. There is so much else to think about besides who takes the next turn, and which card to pull. I can still hear the frustrated voices of my siblings and cousins: "Patty! Your turn! Just pay attention." It's just not that easy. Nothing is.

More times than not, I have attended church without actually "hearing the message."

The church in Oak Park was gloriously beautiful. Angel statues, stained glass, and plaster saints graced every nook of the centuries-old building, and the heady incense filtered through the pews to cast enchantment. I was 24 years old, pregnant for the first time, and feeling not-quite-right in the stifling, artificial heat of the early winter. In pursuit of fresh air, I went out to sit on the stairs until I felt better. Piped through a tinny speaker, the reader's voice came through, clear and crisp as the air on my cheeks. What I heard was life altering. The shepherd must tend his flock. Indeed, I would resign from my teaching job to stay home and care for my baby. And that is what I did.

I went to visit Adrian yesterday. For confidentiality purposes, we have to stay in an industrial visiting room with blue-greenish rubbery couches and a small pile of board games with smashed lids and mismatched pieces. We decided to play Candyland. I noticed the word "bitch" scrawled in brown marker in childish hand on two of the cards. Adrian and I started our game just as a line of "inpatients" marched past the room. They halted at the door to Floor 1 West, and there they remained for what seemed like what would be the entire lunch hour.

"Lila! You can't go to the cafeteria. You have to be here for 24 hours," boomed a voice from beyond. Lila, a sweet-faced girl with long brown hair and wise eyes, and who looked to be middle school age, left the line immediately and spun around in the hall.

"She's new," said Adrian, matter-of-factly.

She peered into our visiting room and joined our game. Since there were only two intact Candy Land markers, we used my Chapstick as another. We took turns, the three of us, and I often had to be reminded to draw my card. Lila shared that she didn't think her mom would come to visit her, that her mom was "disappointed in her." Pretty soon, an attendant shuffled in with some extra lunch trays. Adrian and Lila were poking at their sloppy joes, chocolate pudding, and green beans with very little enthusiasm when David burst into the room. A sturdy boy of about eight years, he looked as if he had been crying. His tray was presented to him, and he went after his food as if he hadn't eaten in days, and talked with great passion about random things as though he had been bursting to share this important news with his captive audience.

When I was student teaching, I was secretly afraid of the "emotionally disturbed" and the "behavior" kids. I was afraid of what they might do to me. But, as I have come to learn, if not to understand, it is not about me. It is, perhaps, about the deep pain and force within that is in no way something that can be controlled and must be met, as impossible as it may seem, with a depth of understanding and compassion.

"Hey, let's play a game," David piped as he scrambled to his feet and pushed some more chairs toward the Candyland station. He could use the Chapstick, and I would just watch. David was first to make it to the Candy Mountain, or wherever you land when you win the game. He got up and walked directly to where Lila was sitting, moving his food-crusted face within inches of hers.

"I just think you're really beautiful," he said, with absolutely no emotion, before moving to find another game.

Lila looked at me, took a deep breath, and told me that she really needed to hear that. Her eyes shone with a new spark that signaled, perhaps in a subtle way, that the first glimmer of healing was taking place. It wasn't in the form of a shot or a behavioral strategy, but from the honest, unsolicited gift of a kind word from, some might say, an unlikely source.

And yesterday, when I was back for my visit, there, too, was Lila's mom, and they were smiling, looking at paint chips together, deciding what fresh shades of pink would look best on her walls at home.

I'm not sure I would have heard the reading this Sunday if I hadn't been riveted to attention by "Ezekiel" passing across the screen. I again heard the words that set me on my journey half a lifetime ago as a young mother. It was the same passage, only now the meaning was much deeper. I will keep tending my flock, I will listen for the music, and I will stay strong on this journey, for my little boy and for my whole flock, because this journey is only the beginning.

The Not-So-Great Hair Experiment:

Ode to a Friend

(February 4, 2015)

I haven't combed my hair for nineteen days. That's before my friend died.

There has to be more to this life.

I knew her from somewhere; I just couldn't place her. Our paths must have crossed at some point during my college years in DeKalb. There must have been something more before that, too, because I have known her from a place within for quite a long time. I came to know her, officially, when I visited babies at her childcare center. She would let me sit in her office as she did a million tasks right before my eyes. When one of the teachers called her, she was quick to take her place among the children, calming a fussy baby or intervening in a toddler squabble. I watched her. She was masterful, and I admired her.

As I walked through the snow to deliver macaroni and cheese dinner to the family yesterday, I was reminded of the day, perhaps eleven or so years ago, when I had been called to visit their little boy for an evaluation. My friend was on her way out the door for gymnastics class with her sparkly-eyed, then six-year-old daughter. Those sparkly eyes flowed with a river of tears as this little girl, now seventeen, dissolved in sadness when we laid her mother to rest last week.

The last time I saw my friend, and in the last conversation I had with her, I told her that I was going to let my hair dread. She was aghast. She wondered why I would ever want to do that. I really had no answer, except that I just thought I would.

After a bit of research and consultations with a couple of people that have dreaded hair, I decided to let nature take its course, to let them form naturally. And every day when I wake up, I wonder if I am doing the right thing. Not just with the hair, but with everything.

I could sense the angels around me with each breath at her funeral. A swirl of incense danced around the head of the baby in my arms. The soulful hymns and an overwhelming sense of grief shook my body, and I was never more grateful to have my husband at my side. I thought of how my friend had held and calmed so many babies, and I watched her husband hold their little son, a boy who had no idea how different his world was going to be from this day forward. My friend lived her life, in the depths of great challenges, as though each moment, and each person in that moment, was the most important of all. We have learned so much from her.

She was gone. Just days before, I had stopped combing my hair. I can't help but wonder if she peers at me with disdain as she holds heaven's babies, protecting them with her untangled, downy angel wings. Actually, I am quite sure she doesn't. I don't think she would even care. Certainly, she wouldn't. She was like that; she loved fully, and she was able to help others find the good in themselves. She also stood up for what she believed, and she was not afraid to speak for herself or for others. She was a true hero, and she leaves a stunned legacy wondering where to find meaning in what has happened.

This ratty hair is starting to drive me crazy. Everything, I know, is a journey. I could honor my friend by combing it out tomorrow morning, or I could march on, as she, perhaps would, without concern, and because we never know what awaits us around the corner.

Rest in peace, dear one. I will be waiting for you to show me some signs. Loud and clear, please.

Nothing and the Birthday Party

(May 14, 2015)

[Photograph of a fortune reading: "This year your highest priority will be your family."]

I didn't really think it would go like that. I had read things, envisioned things. I thought I would feel relieved, or at least find some sort of comfort in knowing that a decision had been made.

Certainly I had known in the moment. Those were such joyful days; those were days full of the mystery of unknown destiny, where you are sure that your dreams will one day be fulfilled, and that the things you hope for and imagine will actually be part of a far-off reality.

In many ways, those wishes and dreams have come true.

There was never a day that I looked to the future and did not see myself as a mom. Perhaps that is why I embraced her so fully, and why she became part of my every breath. She was my little girl, and she was perfect from head to toe. She often wore a little Brownie uniform; there could have been no better-suited outfit for this precious sprite. We had been matched by a service agency; I, as a college student, was to be her "big sister," to spend some time with her on a weekly basis. Our hours together would have been constant if schedules had permitted; I filled my soul with the levity of her laughter amid my anatomy and physiology textbooks and late night beer nugget deliveries. I took her to class with me, read books to her on the stones behind the back entrance to my apartment, took her thrift shopping at every chance, trimmed her soft brown hair, and even took her with me to the 10,000 Maniacs concert in the city. I knew that I had been matched with the ultimate gift in this little person. During those years of finding my way to adulthood, this perpetually smiling child was my grounding force. I loved her thirty-some years ago, as still I do today.

I remember telling her that if anything ever happened to her mom, she could stay with me. She didn't have much of a reaction to my statement. We had been driving in the car, and we probably just turned the music louder and went on to talk about chocolate chip cookies or dandelions or something.

Now, I understand why she couldn't begin to process my offer. She already had a mom, and it wasn't me.

I had known, but I had forgotten. All those years ago. I didn't remember. We had a birthday party for my little sister. The guests, a mix of student friends of mine, a few family members, and several of her friends, climbed the stairs and walked through the musty hallway to apartment # 2, to be greeted by what must have seemed a pink and white wonderland: a cake with kitten decorations, streamers, party hats, a sparkly piñata, and a pile of neatly wrapped presents, all in celebration of this tiny girl, my girl.

But she really wasn't my girl.

It would be easy to take the elevator. I always think this to myself as I begin to climb the marble-looking steps at the county court house. I do like the scenic route, though, wherever I go. I am also afraid of whom I may meet in the elevator. That could be a very long ten seconds. My heart is always racing by the time I reach the benches outside the juvenile court room. Perhaps I am winded from climbing the stairs, but my nerves have certainly come to the surface, raw and vulnerable in anticipation of what is to come. Sometimes, it's a continuance. Other times, it's merely to set a date. On occasion, it is a status change. Rarely, it seems, is it a major decision in the case.

She wouldn't, or perhaps couldn't, look at me. Though I had found myself in this very spot many times before, this time everything was different. My seasoned veteran of a caseworker stood at my side, close enough that I could feel the energy that she had poured into this situation and some of which had been stolen from her very soul. Often, you see, and in this case above others, it is far more than a job, and a thankless one, at that. She is so very good at her life's calling.

I had envisioned, if this moment ever was to come, approaching the judge side-by-side with the woman that had birthed my child, holding her hand for support as she stepped up in her bravest of moments. I had imagined us being strong together, but instead, I wasn't even there.

She didn't want the photos. I debated about bringing them, wondering if it would stir something that was not ready to be exposed. No regrets, just a gift that could not be given. At least, not now.

I didn't know it was her that had been there, at that birthday party, all those long years ago. I didn't remember that my little girl had invited her to play at my college apartment. And I was looking for something else in my photo boxes when I was reminded of the birthday party. My smiling, elfish girl, surrounded on her happy day by a mixture of good-sport college kids in birthday hats and third grade classmates, eagerly anticipating a turn to swing at the piñata, stood alongside a young friend who bears, in this photo, an amazing resemblance to my young son. It took my breath away, because I knew. I knew we had been connected at a deeper level, at a simpler time, and I was keenly aware that through the pain and grief, this was a sort of destiny.

This girl, this friend to my little sister so many years ago, stood strong, if not disconnected, through the confusion, indecision, and evasion of the present moment. She was clear in her intentions, though, as she faced the judge that day, as she surrendered her rights to this child's first birthday party, to his kindergarten send off, to his Mother's Day gifts, to his little league games…to his entire childhood. Perhaps in many ways, she is still her eight-year-old self. Though she could not let me show her on that day in the courtroom, I am so grateful to her, for the gift that I never expected to get. And it wasn't my birthday. My girl, my little sister, had a hand in this gift; too, in the form of certainty, in the form of punctuating my need to know that this is how the stars were supposed to align.

She will be at each and every birthday party. We will not see her, except through the eyes and smile of a small boy, but we will remember this time. We will remember that she is his first mother, and that she will always be important to him, and to us; she will always be the reason for his existence. For that, and for everything, I am grateful.

I know we are the lucky ones on this journey, to have the privilege to care for and nurture these children who indeed remind us to cherish what we have, and to live each day in reverence to something much greater than we ever will be.

Once Upon A Time

(November 22, 2015)

Our bookshelves contain so many volumes and stories that are forever a part of my collection of memories from the early childhood of my little sons.

I am looking for a ladder, not only in the theoretical sense, for one that would let me rise above the stars, to look on my days, and to find the reasons behind all my pursuits. I am also looking for just the right wooden ladder to allow tiny readers (and those of us who can no longer scale a four-foot wall without a boost) access to the shelf of nostalgic wonder, a shelf stocked with all of the best and most important stories. The ladder has to be simple so as to fit without sticking out too far into the hallway. I hope it will have a history, for those are the best kind of things.

I'll take out the first book that catches my eye.

Each day, sometimes many times on a given day, our farmhouse reveals a new possibility for a project. As I walk the property to become more familiar with our land, my dreams flow unharnessed. There is so much here, so much yet to unlock, and so much yet to discover. And when I start just one little thing, it's hard to ignore all the others that beckon so convincingly.

That volume reminded me of another that we loved to read together.

Never have I been a fan of carpet. It had to go, right away, this matted nondescript brownish remnant, which was tacked to that empty nook behind the stairs, next to the rooms where the little boys sleep. I knew just what this space was going to be, what purpose it would serve, even before the previous homeowner had accepted our hopeful bid.

Within a few short weeks of our closing date, the carpet was pulled away like one of the unnecessary book covers I had been required to make from a grocery bag in seventh grade. The beaten pine boards have come to a new life with a coat of sparkly purple paint. One of the bookshelves from our old house just happened to fit in the space as if it had been built in. A soft bench cushion from a precious new friend beckons its first visitor. I just need that ladder.

As the baby slept peacefully in his room down the hall, I took my time opening the cardboard boxes and stocking the shelves with books from a quarter century of childhoods. I knew nearly each book intimately, though it had been many years now since most had been paged through. I could breathe in the text and my mind would fill with the image of a lazy picnic at Wilder Park, or a trip to the Starry Sky with my favorite mama friends, or hours keeping bedside vigil with a feverish boy. Those days, once upon a time, are gone now. Time has gotten the best of me, I realize, with my days a jumble of caseworker visits, fight mediation, and calls from the principal. "Goodnight Moon" does not have the same charm now that someone is swearing at me from the bottom of the stairs.

Sometimes, I wish for a really, really long ladder.

I admire my friend Sonja. She still, in a life that mirrors mine in many ways, finds solace in her books and continues to allow her passion a place on the stage. Sonja has opened my eyes, once again, to this timeless gift; she has reminded me not to forget. She has even bought me some books...books that I am eager to read…once I find my ladder.

There's a tiny boy stirring, and I am going to be sure we have plenty of adventures together in this magical spot.

And right now seems a good time to start.

The Invitation

(March 10, 2016)

He died. Dan showed me the obituary that appeared in the Daily Chronicle.

The plans were crafted with starry eyes and, certainly, a bit of hesitancy. He may not have wanted to be invited back to what had been his home for the last forty years, to what was now our haven, our beloved farm. He may not have wanted to enter where there certainly would have been a cavalcade of memories, where his life partner had lived alongside him, where their children had been raised.

Would he like how the floors turned out, our rich, warm hardwood that sprawls wall to wall throughout the farmhouse, or would he miss the linoleum that bore the marks from the wheels of his desk chair where he sat, for hours on end, pining, maybe, to have back the years, the decades that had caught up to him?

I should have sent the note; there was never going to be a perfect time.

The scream was such that it sliced through my glassy veil, halting my tears even as they fell. He had, minutes before, proclaimed several times that he hated me, and that he wished I wasn't his mother. Near the close of a long, embattled day and separated from Adrian by only a shower curtain, I could no longer hold my emotions. The deep sobs were therapeutic. Then came the scream.

"I got a cut! Under my arm! It stings!" More screams. I looked at the quarter inch wisp of red in his armpit and wondered how the pain could possibly match the horrifying noise he was making.

Just then, he had a revelation. "You did it, Mom, with your fingernail. When I was fighting!"

Indeed, I could have. I must have. And I am so sorry that I did. If I turn my back to stir the soup, to change the baby's diaper, or to answer the door, I can't be sure that I won't be needed to mediate, to intervene. Today, I had to pull him away from the near attack on his sister, from the misinterpretation of misguided laughter, from a one-sided sparring match that is a common occurrence across our days, expected fallout as part of the chaos of parenting my children. In my attempt to hold him to keep him from hurting his sister, I had hurt him. And for that, I am deeply sorry.

My daughter said she was sorry today. That's a big deal for her. She said something that she knew she shouldn't have, and she regrets it.

And maybe I regret never reaching out, never sending the card, and never extending the invitation. Maybe I regret never sitting with him in our living room, looking across the fields, begging stories of this Twombly Road farm from the liveliest place inside of him. Maybe I regret that he wasn't able to stand at the back of the property as my little sons splashed through the puddles, gathered sticks, and climbed the trees. Perhaps he would have seen his own children through mine, with their fleeting joy of childhood that turns, all too soon, to the grind of adult obligation, and perhaps that vision, those memories, could have somehow filled his soul.

I never invited him to the farm, though I had planned to. I never did, and he died. For this, I am sorry.

I had gone out to fill the bird feeders and to finish a few chores. There was something that I hadn't noticed before at the side of the barn. A mass of vines and thatch now played a part in decorating what was barely recognizable as a Christmas tree. Its silver tinsel had long since faded to a mossy brown-green. The thick metal trunk, though, appeared solid and strong. If only there had been something left of the stand to hold it in place. I pulled this old remnant of Christmases past to the curb for the next day's garbage pickup.

I often look back from the street to admire the farm. This time, I noticed the cardinal who had come to perch on the sturdy branch that held the feeder, freshly filled with black oil sunflower seeds. I have heard that a cardinal signals the return of a loved one that has passed.

I knew, then, that he did come back. He didn't need my invitation, for he was always welcome, and he was here to stay.

May he rest in peace, in God's embrace and in the peaceful memories of our shared farm, the best place on Earth.

Happy: Chickens as Teachers

(March 22, 2016)

Though I much prefer a simple afternoon in the garden to one spent at the Magic Kingdom, I still believe that a trip to Disney World is a sort of childhood rite of passage. Having frequented the park with my family as a young vacationer, I have fond memories of drinking Orange Bird slushies and chasing down characters with an autograph book alongside (and in the safety of) my sister and my girl cousins; all of us were wearing pigtails and were dressed in matching striped polyester short suits.

Two days wasn't long enough. I had read and prepared all these months; I even had my homemade isolation brooder ready to meet the needs of sick chickens. When it happened, though, no number of books or trips to the feed store could have been enough to teach me about the sadness in that moment of time. Of course it could…it would happen. All the sources warned us: death is just part of the nature of chicken keeping.

We must have been in our early teen years. I'm not sure my sister

Krista, two years older than me, was excited about family vacations anymore. Krista was instinctively masterful at everything she did. She was fearless, admirable, and a true path-blazer. There we were in Fantasy Land with the rest of humanity in a confetti-like swirl of mouse ears, ice cream, and caramel corn, with the tinny sound of "It's a Small World" rising above the crowd.

It could have been anyone, and it wasn't her fault. On the crowded plaza, Krista somehow collided with a knee-high toddler, accidentally knocking the child to the ground. I still remember the glares…the gasps…the scorn of on looking adults who viewed my sister, in that moment, as someone devoid of compassion. I saw a vulnerable side of Krista, my hero, as her fairy green eyes widened and brimmed with tears. I wanted to help her, to absorb some of the pain that she certainly must have been feeling. I didn't know how.

On the second day, Happy died. She was the baby's chick, and he wouldn't understand anyway. Maybe that would make it easier on everyone. I thought it would be a good idea to burn her remains in the barrel outside. I was hoping to avoid stirring up further trauma in case a wild something would dig up Happy's remains one day. If we burned her, I reasoned, her ashes could be part of the soil of the farm.

"I want to hold her, please," insisted Robin, who, at six, looked barely bigger than the small chick that was wrapped in a soft cloth diaper, a gentle reminder of the sweetness of very early childhood at our home. His tears streamed without barriers, from a place of grief that I had mistakenly thought might not matter as much because it was his baby brother's chicken, not his, that had died.

"Can we bury her in the ground?" Somehow, children know what they need. We wrote a little note for Happy and tucked it, along with her swaddled little body, in an empty granola bar box. Dan dug a hole deep in the ground between two evergreens, and we marked her grave with a wooden block.

I took Robin with me to the grocery store that evening. He seemed uncharacteristically pensive, and then he announced that he missed his other mom. Robin, my small son who had been called only "Boy" when he arrived at my door as a newborn, was missing his birth mom. Though he had never visited or even seen her, the longing was real. The loss of a tiny pet chicken had stirred this deepest of wounds. I could acknowledge this, and I could tell him what I knew, but there is much left unsaid and unanswered, for all of us.

The day the chickens came, I had a visit from Theresa, my high school friend whom I have known for 35 years. The brightness of her soul and the gift of her friendship even through the distance in physical presence has been a source of comfort for me across college years, early motherhood, and the trials of our mutual transitions from our nests. We had spoken of our losses and lessons as we shared bagels and cookies and introduced each two-day-old chicken to the brooder. In your shared experiences, you become part of that person, and they become part of you.

I received a message from my daughter's birth mother today. She thanked me for being a good mother to her daughter. This is a gift that I never expected to receive. This love, these burdens, these unexpected life lessons are powerful, more so than I could have imagined. Holding the grief, the hurt, and the confusion of another, acknowledging it just so they know you are there, must be enough when it's all we have: the connection, the common ground, the acknowledgement, can make softer what we don't really understand. When I don't know why, surely it is helpful to have someone to sit by my side. That must be much bigger than any words.

When I returned to the Magic Kingdom with my own family, the Orange Bird was gone. Strappingly romantic heroes courting sparkly, flowy-haired princesses with waists the size of pennies had all but replaced Daisy Duck and Thumper. The magic wasn't the same as when I was a little girl, when I rode Space Mountain for the first time with my brave sister. It was still magic, though, for my little ones, because this is all they knew. I miss that Orange Bird.

And though we miss Happy, we are grateful for the powerful gifts she gave and the lessons she taught during her brief time with us. We are learning that we can't always be with those that we love, but that we can feel more deeply through our experiences. Maybe we truly don't know what we miss until the realization comes in the form of our emotions, seeping through the tears of vulnerability to a greater understanding of ourselves.

Our chicken keeping adventures are already much more than pictures in a book. The reflections into ourselves offered by another, the power of true companionship, and the acceptance of the things about which we have no control will be lessons as valuable, and even more, than the experience of gathering that highly anticipated first fresh egg. And that's magic.

••

Since we have moved to the farm, traveling my walking paths first requires a trip to town or to the university. I believe I have done this exactly two times in the past year. The simplicity of farm chores does offer similar thinking space, enhanced by its naturescape, though it does nothing to combat my rolls of overindulgence. I steal the time that I can, digging alongside the chickens, until I am jolted to attention by the baby monitor. Soon, one of the gardening chores will be to create a walking path through the twists of boggy grasses, brush, and overgrowth at the back of the property.

I am secretly curious about many things. Maybe we choose not to ask the questions or not to talk about things because we don't know if it is okay. Still, though, we remain, curious and awkward, as we look for true meaning. And in the answers, we find more questions.

It is still a rare Sunday morning that I make it to church with the little boys. I am still trying to get the message. When the crazy overwhelming stuff happens, I know I need to look at the little details to get me to the next minute, to the next hour, and to the next day. When I hold that breath to notice the visiting hummingbird or the way my daughter Hope puts her gentle hand on Adrian's shoulder at just the right time, it is then that I am reminded that none of this is about me, nor is it up to me. The real meaning, though, is in what we come across every day.

Sometimes, there are no questions. My friend showed me a sign. In the wake of the goodbyes, when the grief was still raw, and though she was no longer of this earth, she had something to offer. It was welcome as a homemade casserole or a bunch of daisies in winter. When I opened the door to check for the bus, there to greet me on my front porch was a perfect heart of freshly fallen snow. I knew right away that it came from her. When I am missing my friend, I can think about the time that I had with her, and I can have a good cry, all the while knowing that she stands alongside those to whom she was dear.

After eighteen months without combing my hair, I still wonder. My dreads are more defined by now, but they have shrunk to a fraction of their original length. Sometimes, it does feel like we are moving backwards, going in the wrong direction. If we give up, though, we will never, ever know. The strength, just as the signs, will be there.

I still see my little sister. We share Thanksgiving dinner or pizza at the kitchen table, and I am grateful after the passing of years, of decades, that her sparkle still lights my days. I see her spirit in some of my children, and I know we all belong together, no matter how we have arrived here. There will be a place, too, for others, who will always be in our thoughts and welcomed into our home, if that day should come. I wonder sometimes what it would be like if the tables were turned, and if it were me looking in from outside. I wonder, and wonder some more, always with a breath and a heartbeat for what might have been.

My second- hand ladder is now in place. It was the perfect size, and a cherry-mahogany match to the bookshelf which fit into the reading loft with maybe half-an-inch to spare.

I didn't use all of the peat moss when I filled the chickens' dust bath which we built inside the run. One of my chickens created her own place to roll in the mud, at the side of the barn where a stone had been removed. That place, then, became another dust bath and home to the leftover peat moss. A hydrangea would be perfect here, too, to provide for my chickens some shelter from the sun. The other side of the path to the barn would make the perfect haven for the fairy garden, the one that has been envisioned at least a hundred times, the one whose cast iron elves, tiny stepping stones, miniature rusty metal watering can, sparkly moon rocks, and spotted toad stools have been waiting to reveal themselves. As for my little Joey, he loves to be in the garden, to chase the chickens, and to drive the little cars, as did his big brothers in days past. He also brings me books, without concern for the special reading spot or the ladder. I have another chance to go back to the magic.

And with the children back at school, I am able to use Joey's naptime to work on some of these visions in the yard. With each shovelful of spent foliage that I add to the burn pile, and with each tiny perennial that sinks into this rich soil, I am conscious of the change, that this becomes more our farm every day. As we are comfortable, we also remember the connection, and how we, too, are just here on this earth for a short time, to spin a tiny tale all our own.

Lessons have certainly come hand-in-hand with chicken keeping. We are gathering at least half a dozen eggs every day, and my Robin is the best chicken helper. I may lose sight of him for a time, only to find him running toward me, hands cupped and eyes sparkling, as he announces, "chicken egg!" For this, and for so many other reasons, is why we are here.

WHAT WE LOVE COMES BACK TO US

We want to hold our best treasures close to us, to keep them neat and tidy so we can feel just right. Then, as we march on through our days, we look back to see that we are a little bit different. I can't keep my little boys small forever. I can only watch to see what is in store for us all.

Something that was meaningful was taken from me. The many children that have come to my home have experienced loss in the deepest sense, and their stories can give us hope.

I have written of my love for the great game of baseball which cannot stand still. My ten-year-old fastball pitcher has, at 22, long since hung up his cleats as he stands at the brink of adulthood, watching the game from the sidelines. My six-year-old, though, is looking forward to his first season of little league come this spring.

There is a tale of a visiting butterfly, a sign for so many things, a story of embracing what we have of our days, of our looming goodbyes, of the end of life of our beloved grandma, and the beginning of what is to come as my children step off into adulthood.

There is a story of a longtime friend, of how our encounters over the years have surely been guided by a higher power, and my story of fancy, sparkly little animals and how I am reminded that I will again be with those that I love.

Through the memory of a trip back to the town where Dan grew up, I have come to understand that our experiences can have different, but equally important meaning to another person. And what we do love will be part of us and will come back to us in due time.

The Brightest Star
(March 5, 2014)

I loved having my own apartment in college. I once lived above the old Star Furniture building, which has many years since been razed and is now a park, complete with fountain. My landlord sent a young man to "paint my bathtub" while I was away one day. My cassette player went missing that day, but what was contained within, my bootleg tape of Natalie Merchant and Tracy Chapman's "Souls Never Die" was also never again seen. This left me with a sense of deep violation. I often tell my children, in the throes of their tattling and bossing: "worry about yourself." When my song was taken from me, all I really had to do was to worry about myself. Maybe, because that was all I had, it hurt much more.

A call came from the school today describing some unsettling behavior of my foster daughter. There is no way to see inside the baggage that she carries on a daily basis; to really know the battles she has fought, and the songs that she has lost, in her tiny, tumultuous lifetime.

Mine takes a breath as I wait for the sigh that never sounds.

I am coming to learn that sometimes, good stuff goes away. That doesn't mean that it will never come back. My first son, Jonathan, was entering his teenage years when we began our fostering journey. In my early journal pages, I often described Jonathan as "full of wonder," "wise," or "of the stars." His deep, intense eyes have always been portals to something extraordinary. At twenty-two, he is pursuing his path as a neuroscience researcher. Jonathan recently spoke to a group of prospective foster parents. When asked to reflect on his experiences growing up in a foster home, he had this, among other things, to say:

"Many foster children have been hurt, and their emotional scars are often apparent. They take the form of impatience, selfishness, isolation, and roaring outbursts. It is not difficult to notice these unhealthy patterns of thought and behavior. But a moment's thought will reveal that these extreme examples are caricatures of your own inner life."

We are these people.

God, it's dark outside. Where did they go? I opened the door, but nobody was left inside. I'm going to look for them, and then they will find me. My own child has helped to identify things in me that I did not know were there. I think of just how much that song on my cassette meant to me in 1988, and it makes me think of the brokenness that swirls through every cell of some children who have entered our home...cold, hungry, with hallowed eyes. And most did not, could not even cry. They had been ripped from their familiar, from what they had known, and from all they had been. For me, just one song. For them, the whole world. No wonder there are behaviors.

Clear the thoughts; rub your eyes. It's almost time to fly, fly. Go forth, my first, and make them see you.

It's really easy to find music on the internet (even for me). That rare compilation is once again at my fingertips. I didn't know if I would hear it again. I don't know if there will be healing, if the burdens will lighten. As the seasons turn and Jonathan moves, potentially, across the country, I will keep holding the hope by moving through each day, trying my best to live the advice of my boy: to see myself in others, and to look beyond the behaviors to know that we really are here together, and that what we most miss will always be part of us. And... that we will probably hear our best song again.

Photo credit to my dear friend, Catherine Finn, who took this picture when these were the littlest and biggest boys in our tribe!

It's Just a Game

(April 25, 2014)

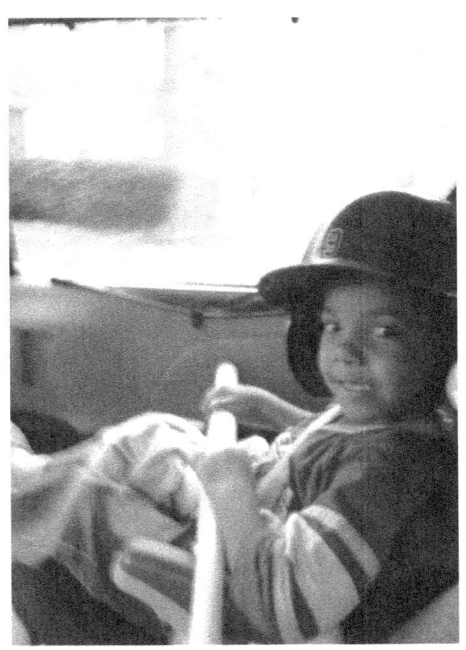

My Wilson "Catfish Hunter" glove, still adorned with my name in purple bubble letters, takes its place of honor on the top shelf in our mudroom. One of the ties is quick to come loose; I can still recall the salty taste of the leather as I waited for a token ball to come my way in the right field corner. I was probably in fourth or fifth grade when I first thought of baseball as something other than a really boring sport that my dad watched on television. My brother, three years younger than me, was never really taken by the game. I sat, one day, on the not-yet-rotted side of the wooden bleachers at the little league field, trying to make sense of what was happening to my brother and to the other boys on the diamond. In plain view was the creek where, as the story goes, my young neighbor had been arrested for relieving himself. On that day, though, I was looking for meaning in what was unfolding before me. The young pitcher, all of eight years old, tossed a ball in the general vicinity of the batter. Sometimes the batter did not swing the bat. Sometimes he did. Once he missed, and the other times, he hit the ball, but not in the direction of where the fielders were positioned. After a while, he made his way, rather slowly, to first base. This, I deduced, was because he did a pretty good job hitting the ball. Later, I recalled this scene and realized that the batter had merely taken a base-on-balls. I had a lot to learn.

The game became increasingly important to me, and I evolved, rather quickly and much to my father's delight, into a Cubs fan. Manny Trillo, unsung second baseman that he was, rose as my hero. I baked a little cake for #19 and delivered it to Wrigley Field one summer. A few days later, while babysitting, I was spellbound as I struggled to understand the words coming through my end of the phone. "Thank you for the cake. I only eat the vanilla. I don't like the chocolate."

Never much of an athlete, I was generally content to fill my soul with baseball by listening to the radio. Once or twice each summer, extending across decades, my dad would take me to Wrigley Field. As a young mother, I looked forward to this reprieve from my daily rhythm as a child looks forward to the magic of Christmas day. We would always stop for Thai food before the game, and, certainly, we would find Starbucks for the drive home. I am happy that I was not aware that our last such ritual was indeed that: the last.

James had an incredible arm for pitching as a very young boy. His brief stint at t-ball offered no indication that he held such promise. As a four-year-old, he only stood behind the screen and declared, "I'm not doing this."

Life took hold, and we moved to DeKalb. A few seasons passed before James joined park district baseball. He had a fierce and powerful throw, and he loved the game as I did. We played baseball in the early spring through October, and we couldn't quite get enough. The leaves were falling at a clip, and the last game was upon us. There had been some whispering back and forth among the coaches, and a small boy approached the plate. The pitcher had been instructed to walk this kid, and that he did. The little boy did not have long to live, and he was made to feel like a baseball hero, for sure, on that fall Sunday.

I hadn't seen the signs. Shortly after the season finished, James began having some health challenges of his own. In January, the doctors found a brain tumor. At that time, we didn't know if James would survive.

He did. He had many more baseball seasons. And one day, it was all over. He was just done; he wasn't interested any more. And it wasn't up to me. It was just a game.

Last week, the little boys and I stopped at McCormick Park. We tried to beat the rain. Wiffle balls, duct-taped bat, and old softball glove in hand, we took the field. In the blink of an eye, our "caboose" will be ready to play shortstop. I will be there watching from the bleachers, and I can't wait.

Chaos and Butterflies

(August 11, 2014)

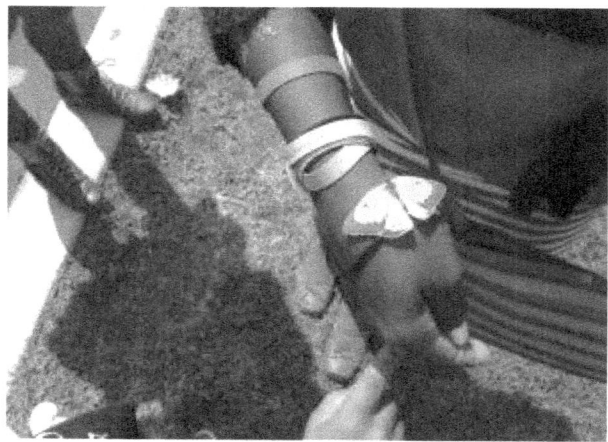

I didn't notice the butterfly; my mind was racing toward too many other things. We filed from the van, hoping to be ready for something for which there could be no adequate preparation. As I entertained visions of hollow eyes lining the hallway and the overwhelming smell of something slipping away, my presence was clearly elsewhere. It was one of my girls, and then the other, that extended hands as welcome perches for the sunshine yellow butterfly. Passed from one youthful hand to another, to a tiny boy and back again, the small butterfly lifted its wings ever so slightly as it was set to rest, seemingly perfectly content, on the reddest flower in an urn of bright and mighty annuals which nearly beckoned the heavens. A man of eighty-something, slumped to one side of his vinyl-and-metal push cart, stared past my children, and the butterfly, but I know he saw everything.

After an hour of off-key camp songs offered to comfort or, at least, soften the crawl of the afternoon's clock; curious wanderers scouting out a good time and inviting themselves to join our circle of activity, hoping to find whatever meaning there might be left to find; pleas for help ("let me out!"); and feelings that this could be our last time visiting grandma, we are going to get a pizza. As the sliding door opened and the summer air mixed with emotions that had no definition, I saw that the butterfly had gone.

My son could have been a small child, his nearly six-feet-four-inch frame curled to rest on the twin-size mattress on our basement floor. Here he is, for ten days, on the bridge between his childhood and the future's unknown. He has left home, he has done university studies, he has lived in his own apartment. But this time, he will travel thirty-two hours by car to pursue his passion. He will not be home for Labor Day weekend. He will not be home for Thanksgiving. He will be in California for five years, which is more time than his youngest brother has lived. I support him wholeheartedly, and the angst of letting go is, as are the feelings that brew within my soul at the nursing home, indefinable.

Another son is packing up his coffee machine, towels, frying pan, Frisbee, and even the coveted velvet estate sale love seat that his older brother cannot take on his journey. This boy is returning to college, moving to a house with his friends. Today, the mounds of laundry, displaced chairs, and random piles of paper that clutter our bungalow are strongly reminiscent of the chaos that certainly fills my brain. I don't remember a time where more transitions loomed, bringing with them unwelcome gifts including anxiety, overwhelming sadness, and a sense of pining for where I have gone before. There, too, is great joy in realizing that this is actually what is supposed to happen. Your children are destined to grow strong, and to find their wings, one way or another, and for however long.

I have a wise friend who has taught me much about the value of simplicity, the beauty of nature, and the importance of sharing these gifts with our very youngest. With visions of milkweed and monarch butterflies, Sarah's gentle stories and actions bring a bit of peace to my tumultuous thoughts of recent days as she teaches, perhaps even without words, of the parallel between loving so hard, so fiercely, and letting go, while taking time to notice the glorious beauty of the wings.

Today, I am grateful for my friend, for my dear ones, for one more visit to see Grandma, and for the hope that I may remember that there is so much more for each and every one of us. I am remembering the sweet days when I was all that my three little boys needed, and I now have no choice but to embrace the passage of time and move onward, just as they do when they are ready to fly.

Au Revoir

(December 5, 2014)

How I loved high school French class. I never gave a thought to how useful it may have been to learn to speak Spanish before embarking on a career in the service field. Once, though, I did attempt to use my French "skills" to converse with a West African family as I administered the Battelle Developmental Inventory on their premature twins. It was when they spoke perfect English (with a magnificent French accent) back to me that I knew that my days of interpreting, and my hopes of being bilingual, had come to an abrupt halt.

I can still repeat some of the canned ALM French dialogues that I practiced incessantly with "mon frere" and "ma soeur." I remember making "choux a la creme" with Brother Michael and the rest of the French Club in the basement of a fancy high rise in Oakbrook Terrace. It was great fun dreaming of visiting Paris with Mlle. LeBlanc and my comrades from Catholic high school. I am pretty sure, though, that most of us entered the service field.

I did visit one of my college roommates while she studied at Aix-en-Provence. We spent the same semester abroad; I stayed with a British family in London, where I frequented Camden Market, ate at Windmill Wholefoods, and hunted for Doc Martens. As I waited for my friend to finish in the classroom, I discovered a quaint rose park, espresso, noisette loaves, and the soulfulness that comes from spending idle hours alone, thinking and writing, wrapped in the lush solitude of the graceful spring air. I never did make it to Paris.

All of the students gathered in the same hotel for one night before dispersing via the underground, by taxi, or, most coveted: a ride in the host family's car. Laura shared my hotel room that evening. She also shared my curling iron, and, since she was the first to use it, she was the one to set her long brown hair on fire. We had much to learn as young travelers.

We have connected many times throughout the years. Upon returning to Illinois and resuming my post at the record store, I often saw Laura when she came to the store with her boyfriend, Sam, who had been a longtime customer. We graduated and marched on with our lives.

It wasn't long after Dan and I moved back to DeKalb that we attended a dinner for adoptive families at an Indian restaurant. Across the table, eagerly awaiting a baby from Guatemala, were Laura and Sam.

Our friendship involved the annual Christmas card exchange, an occasional cup of tea, and a chance encounter or two over the years. I knew she was around, but we were busy on both sides. Then, somehow, my fourth grade foster daughter landed in the seat right next to Laura's "baby" at the elementary school. The girls became fast friends. Laura's sweet girl could see beyond the layers of anger, fear, and pain. She could offer what I have often taken for granted: true friendship.

Perhaps there are people, places, or things that we would not like to see again, that we would prefer not to revisit. During my most self-conscious and anxiety-ridden years of high school, I must have been in a hurry to get the best square dance partner. Miss Love blew her whistle, and the boys and girls stood at attention on opposite sides of the gym. She blew it again, and I was first to move toward the line of boys. I was sure I would end up with a good partner this time. I kept going. She blew it a third time. Uh oh. I stopped and turned around, only to see that none of the other girls had moved. Completely humiliated, I made my way back to the line of whispering girls. I do not miss high school gym class at all.

When I took the little boys to Anderson Hall for a gym class, I entered through a side door. The smell of colored pencils, really sharp, brand new ones, came to me clear as the day I had bought them for my drawing class. Twenty-some years earlier, I had entered through the same door, sat on the same couch, and opened my pencils.

Her eyes sometimes break from mine, and she looks off into the distance for a bit. If I speak to her, she might mumble something, or she may have no words at all. I am sure that she has been reminded of something that came before, something that happened during her early years, years when things were uncertain. There was still love. There was still good. There just wasn't enough. Now, when it comes back to her, when she sees it again, she must acknowledge it to remember who she is, lest she forget, and lest we never know.

The rows of Rubbermaid containers, complete with masking tape and Sharpie labels, are stacked nearly to the ceiling in the laundry room. A nostalgic mama and years of fostering have saved many late night shopping trips. It was in the "shoes 9-4" bin that I found the little Doc Martens that the big boys had worn more than a decade before. They would be perfect for Adrian's fancy outfit for Grandma's funeral. There was comfort, a promise from the shoes of a little boy, in knowing that when we say "goodbye," we will, indeed, see her again. There, too, is comfort in knowing that when the sun sets, it will shine for another. I don't really want to go to Paris anymore, but I am happy to sit among the roses and to drink espresso alongside my friend.

Sparkly Things and Fancy Little Animals

(December 30, 2015)

I have no idea when the fascination first began. It was never really an obsession, but rather something that I would allow myself to think of from time to time. My mind would wander to some sort of enchanted place where dogs would be smiling and wearing overalls, lambs would ride little bicycles with bunches of flowers in their handle baskets, and mother cats dressed in Sunday finery would push ivory wicker carriages that held twin kittens tucked beneath sweetly embroidered cotton blankets.

The escalating turns of a little boy sparring match from around the corner bring me back to the present. Later that evening, the dull ache in my hip and the scratch marks on my forearm remind me that my eight year old son will only get bigger and stronger, and that there will come a day when I can no longer hold him to keep us all safe from the tempest of his writhing body. In that moment earlier in the day, though, we were able to weather the storm at hand.

It takes a bit of might and determination to will the tears back as I think of his smallness in the wake of his overwhelming angst, and how things will have to be different when he grows older. I cannot hold that thought, though, because right now, just as the ducks sit cross-legged for a picnic of buttered croissants and strawberries on the clover-massed lawn, all is peaceful and well.

Our young mom coffee shop meet ups evolved over the years, and our beloved Starry Sky has long since closed. My family moved away. It seemed in the blink of an eye, my longtime friend Susanne's toddlers turned to teenagers with their own games and recitals. My older sons, too, were scarcely available when we were able to find time, usually at a bookstore somewhere between our two towns, to catch up over an afternoon latte.

There was always a baby (or maybe two) in tow on my end, and I was always grateful for Susanne's capable extra hands. I would see the fancy little animals, the ones with pinafores and bunches of flowers, for sale at the bookstore, and I would admire them, out loud, and my friend knew. She always did.

As a young teenager and beyond, I looked forward to my babysitting jobs as one of my peers might look forward to a homecoming dance or a trip to the mall. I spent hours reading to my sweetest charges, two darling little boys. The younger boy would wait for me to turn the page and then point an eager toddler finger at the tiniest animal he could find. Every time, and every page. I don't remember if I ever told his parents about that. This little boy, too, loved small things. I hope he still does.

Our Chicago friends gave us a gift certificate to the bookstore a few years ago. When I had found the perfect family book with some funds to spare, I bought myself one of those fancy little animals that were so much a part of my stolen reveries. It was, after all, 25% off.

In the dark shadows on the hardest days, again I fight the demons along with the tears as I consider that when you live among those with mental illness, and maybe you also may not be far from a ledge of sorts, you need the little things.

A padded yellow envelope arrived from Susanne a few days before Christmas. Inside was one of the tiny animals from the bookstore. A little curly lamb, dressed in a pink sundress and seated proudly on a red train, now holds a place of honor on my kitchen windowsill and will forever be a reminder of the whimsy and delight that truly can be part of every day.

When we hope for something, when we love something, we have to believe, and we have to know, that one day, perhaps not even during this time on earth, that that something will come back to us, and we will know it, and it may even be wearing fancy sparkles.

Waiting For It

(April 5, 2016)

Today is opening day, except it is not exactly "opening day," since the Cubs play on the west coast, and the game does not start until nine o'clock tonight. It seems like I have waited a million winters for baseball to begin again. And today, or tonight, the wait will end.

She didn't even know about Happy Joe's, much less the older boys' tradition of cashing in their arcade winnings for hundreds of the best melty butter mints that cost one ticket each. Though she had been to Galena once for her Grandma's funeral, she didn't know its best secrets. She didn't know this city like I did, and she certainly didn't know it like Dan did. When our daughter said she wanted to visit the town where Dan grew up (and which had been the site of many family gatherings over the years, well before this child became part of our family), I was eager to make it happen for her.

He was most everything that I wasn't, and it didn't take long for me to love him. On the day we met, Dan was doing ballet leaps in the streets of DeKalb as we made our way to the Eagles Club which now, from what I understand, might be a swingers club. We went there at the blind matchmaking request of a mutual friend, to see a band and, perhaps in the back of my mind, to forge a future, if it were to be. That night, I started looking for signs.

We packed the Toyota with our five youngest children, our overnight bags, and the hope that there would be some magic left to share with a little girl who we wanted so desperately to carve into our hearts.

I think it was early summer the first time Dan took me home to meet his mom and to see the town where he grew up. We visited the Kandy Kitchen, and he took me to dinner at The Kingston Inn where he had worked as a singing waiter during high school and college summers. I wondered, then, what our future would hold.

The children each chose a bag of sweets and stood at the fudge bar where we, too, had waited to pay for our candy some twenty-seven years before. The sun was warm and bright; almost summer weather for the end of March. We walked a block or two further, past some vaguely familiar shops which beckoned passers-by with samples of popcorn, displays of glistening crystals, and the season's first iced latte. We stopped to get a photo of the "Tokyo House," the restaurant which now occupies the space where Dan had entertained townies and tourists.

Standing with two of my nine children, high on top of a hill in Illinois, I wondered how I had arrived there, barely recognizable under a mop of dreaded hair and fifteen-turned-to-almost-thirty extra pounds of emotional eating, looking out at the same town that had brought me my love. The children were having a great time at Happy Joe's. The girls spent their arcade tickets on butter mints, just as our older boys had done years before. The little boys watched the train circle the dining room as they sat in the booth and ate pizza, just as our older boys had done years before. In their youth and innocence, this was their Galena. And it was just as beautiful as mine.

The sign which once hung outside the Kingston Inn now graces, in quite a weathered state, the wall in our family room. I happened upon the sign when an acquaintance who had known the restaurant's owner offered it for sale. This, like so many other things, was meant to be. It was a true sign, a reminder that those experiences that have been meaningful will find their way back.

My dad is solely responsible for inspiring my love of baseball. Tomorrow, he will have his pacemaker replaced; the signs are there that tell him the time has come. We wait for it, and the time comes. We look back, and it has been the blink of an eye. Inside this window of time is so much to share, so much to look forward to, and so much to pass along.

A new season is here, and with it comes the promise of a long summer of our best game, the treasures of passing on our stories to our little ones, and, of course, some treats from our favorite candy store to savor for just a while longer.

■■■

To be sure, we cannot get inside the pain of another. We can, though, offer what we have. My brother somehow tracked down a recording of my missing musical collaboration. Though my cassette was long gone, he was able to use technology to bring it back to me. The sound quality was much higher, the but the nostalgic gratification was immeasurable.

I am still finding my way to Wrigley Field, even without my dad. Last year, it was James who surprised me with tickets. This season, I took Hope to her first Cubs game along with my friend Laura and her daughter, Hope's friend.

Robin has two t-ball seasons under his belt. Next year, it's on to little league. Though his best skill may be scaling the backstop, there will be reason to, once again, take the field.

Last week, Alice invited me to bring Joey to an activity circle at a nearby nursing home. Residents sat around the perimeter of the room, and parents and toddlers played with toys and kept company. I couldn't help but think of Dan's mom, and I am sure that the residents were reminded of children from years past. There was plenty of sparkle on that Monday morning, as we, across generations, leaned on one another for what had been and for what was yet to be.

Austin left yesterday after spending two months at the farm. He flew back to England to continue his studies, to look for what his future holds. To prepare for the next homecoming, I was tidying up the room where he had spent the last part of summer. "I'm going to play with these," announced Robin, as he pulled a basket from under the bed. Conscious of the time, I called to Robin to make sure he was getting ready for school. He had taken my fancy little animals onto the top bunk, and there were four of them, lined up nice and neat. The lamb that Susanne had sent to me was in the line. Though it's tiny pinafore was nowhere to be found, I knew right then that Robin was appreciating the objects of my great delight in his very own way.

I think we need to make another trip to Galena. These grocery store peanut butter cups do not exactly feed my soul. As the weather turns, I reflect back to the night when I stayed up for this season's first Cubs game. Now, as the calendar winds down, October baseball is a reality. I, along with my dad (whose heart is once again in strong working order) and Cubs fans from a century before, have waited a very, very long time for this, which is sure to be the year.

DISCOVERING GRACE IN THE EVERY DAY

Sometimes the big picture is just too big, too foreboding, and too much to bear. It is then that I remind myself of the little things, the blue marble that shows itself atop the rusty garden gate, and the chocolate chip zucchini bread delivered by a friend, for those bits of grace are what fuel the course of the journey, one small day at a time.

I share my story of how the comfort of my Catholic childhood has stayed with me, even carried me, and how God's presence is revealed to me in the simplicity of nature's offerings or an encounter with a child. Here, too, is the story of a well-loved carnival animal and the tiny boy that chose it to love, above all others.

There is grace in my backyard garden; for it is there that I have left my worries to the fairy roses and lavender stalks. There is the story of a discarded metal circle, found by my son, and how this represents the mystery of those around us. I have written, too, of our own little sources of inspiration, of how I prefer a special silver fork or how my daughter leaves one pant leg tucked into her sock, on purpose, and how we each may feed our souls with spoons that are very, very different.

The grace may come from within, where, with our patterns deep inside, lies the magic -- the magic that makes us who we are, who we have always been, and the magic for who we are yet to be.

There are tales of the push-away rejection of attachment disorder and the feelings left in the wake of an angry outburst, and the grace found in the chance to once again visit parks and ice cream shops with a trio of tiny boys.

Though the bricks crumble, they hold our house firmly on the ground. There is grace, too, of the greatest kind, in hearing a distant child say, "I love you."

What I Know About God
(February 26, 2014)

Conflict is something that I prefer to avoid. There have been times when I have said what I needed to say, and, though I have made people angry at least two times in my adult life (likely many times more, but I will never know), I have felt better for releasing the bottled angst which had stirred within. It is foreboding to express the unspoken, but the unleashing of swirling, resurfacing thoughts must certainly be a necessary step on this journey. And with that premise, I step off.

I miss the saints and angels of my Catholic childhood. The breathtaking beauty of the statues and stained glass captured my attention long after the words to the sermon began to fade on a given Sunday. Try as I did, and still into my adulthood, I find it hard, week after week, to "get the message." I have gotten messages, plenty of messages. But did I get "the message?" Just as a song has new meaning to each discriminating ear, "the message" has been handed down for interpretation. God is, for me, all around.

There is comfort in the familiar. During my semester abroad, somewhere on the outside edge of childhood, just about to make my first footprints as an adult, I found strength and solace in my longstanding Sunday ritual. Whether in Vienna, London, or Aix-en-Provence, I was able to breathe in the beauty before me, and to feel how richly I was blessed.

My family moved to the Chicago area from St. Louis when I was six. The burning question remains a vivid memory: it was our choice, and we were in charge of our destiny. "Do you want to go to the school where you wear uniforms and get out at 2:30pm; or do you want to go where you wear whatever you want but have to go to Sunday school?" I am still not really sure if my mother had been hoping for one response over the other, but we chose, resoundingly, the Catholic school. My first grammar lesson in Mrs. Dunbar's reading group left me flailing with confusion and uncertainty. In perfect Palmer penmanship, she wrote "o-n" at the top of the chalkboard. "Ahn," she read. Wait, doesn't that say "awn?" Do they have some sort of accent here in Illinois, because that is not how we read "on" in St. Louis? I told my mother that I wanted to go back to America where I belonged.

I've never been much for history. The memories that I have carried away from my high school class, "America Since 1945" do not involve the Bay of Pigs or the resignation of President Nixon. I do remember Mr. Barry's characteristic snip-knit ties, and the film where John F. Kennedy proclaimed, "that's good chowder, Bobby." In the same spirit, then, I find it infinitely challenging to read, with any depth of understanding, from the Bible. I do remember, though, when I saw the face of Mary on my bathroom wall.

I must have been giving one of the babies a bath. I was a young mother. Perhaps it was how the sunlight shone through the curtain and reflected onto the wall. But it hadn't been there before, and I haven't seen it since, nor do I remember many details from the vision.

There must be something about the bathroom. On a barren winter day more than nine years ago, I was at home alone with my then ten-year-old son, James. Just three days earlier, James had surgery to remove the culprit that had been wreaking havoc in his body during most of his fourth grade year. My standout pitcher had what was surely a block-long length of hospital gauze wrapped around his precious head. It was up to me, his mom, to clean the wound at the first bath. As the water ran and the bubbles multiplied, I pulled apart the bandage, ever so gingerly, with shaking, unprepared hands. As the last edge fell away, something transcendent was revealed to me. James has a seven-inch scar framing his head, nearly headband-style, that is these days just evident after a fresh buzz cut. It's the only lasting evidence of what was a parent's deepest darkness: the discovery of a little son's brain tumor. On that cold January day in 2005, I saw God through James. There was the crown of thorns perched atop his head, stitches protruding and blood crusted through what was left of his hair. James was carrying my burdens, and through that great trial I have been led to forever believe that much abides, and it will be manifest at the most unlikely opportunity.

As a teenager, I was part of the "Sister's Club." This was a small group of girls that assisted at the convent which was adjacent to the high school. We busied ourselves doing such things as washing the marble steps and wheeling the aging nuns around the chapel. I had a special little nun, Sr. Eleanor, who would fret each afternoon as I handed her a chocolate. She let me know that she had everything that she needed, though I am not sure that I understood what she meant at the time. Regardless, though, I saw the work of God in her holy face.

I have been a restless girl. For me, spirituality continues to be a journey. As the hand of God may guide and the spirit may deliver, I know there is something bigger, something extraordinary, and something ever-so-personal, which fills our souls and brings us the gilded moments of fanfare in the simple calm of the garden path, and the moments of stolen solitude amid the chaos of every given day.

He Looks Loved

(February 21, 2014)

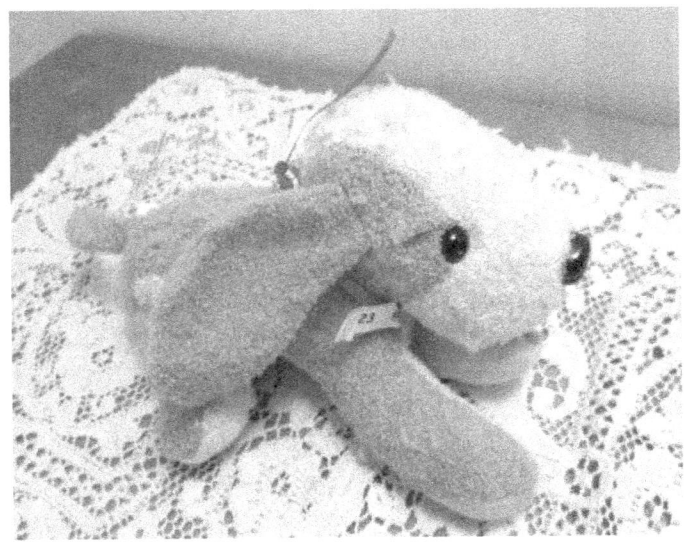

I don't think I like change. How can that be, really? As a college student, I changed my major no less than four times. Dan and I have lived in five houses, thus far, during our tenure as homeowners. And we have had a total of twenty-two children coming and going through our doors in as many years of parenting. Each time I go to the Mediterranean restaurant downtown, though, I choose the very same spinach pie. There is comfort in the present moment, and that, really, is all we have.

We are, once again, rearranging the bedrooms. (I am sorry Dan, and I love you so much). Two years ago at Christmas time, I took four of the children to a party hosted for foster families in the surrounding areas. Each child was allowed to choose a stuffed animal from an overwhelming pile of discards and donations from generous citizens. Some animals were sparkly, fresh, and fluffy, some not so much, but each was tied with a ribbon and marked by a number. Robin, our caboose (a term coined by Dan, not me), barely three at the time, was quite decisive. He smiled smugly as he raised his tiny doggie for me to see. Having been loved already well past his dollar-store value, this little creature was about to get a new life. As I looked at the scuffed, dirty, crusty, and pilling little dog, reminiscent of an elusive prize in a crane-claw arcade game, I thought it was curious that such a thing would be donated for a Christmas party in this condition. My tiny boy, though, found it to be the choice of the pile, the best-in-show.

As I pulled the last few unmatched socks from Robin's dresser to prepare for its move into the hall, there he was: Animal #23, peeking at me with those chipped, beady eyes. "I have been through it, and I deserve your respect and your love. Don't even think of putting me in the 'pass along' bag." And so Animal #23 moved, along with the matched socks and folded Thomas the Tank Engine underwear, into the big boy dresser.

I was shopping yesterday, and Robin was his usual spritely, energetic self. He pulled a package of Unisom from the shelf as I signed for his brother's prescription. "Mom, can I get this?" Though I secretly thought it might be a grand idea, I urged him to put it back on the shelf. "Okay," he piped as he skipped along, replacing the box and making his way to the vitamin bottles for a little rearranging. "He looks loved," said the clerk. I cannot stop thinking about those words. That is the essence of why I am here on this earth. To celebrate, to respect and to love. And I am thankful that I have been reminded of my task at hand, which is not nearly finished.

I have been to Rockford many times during the years. The neurologist is in Rockford; the sleep doctor is in Rockford; court is in Rockford; the best shoe store is even in Rockford. I prefer to take the back roads, where there are as many cows as cars, and plenty of stretches of country pastures, perfect for stirring my thoughts. There is a fence running along much of the many-mile stretch heading into Cherry Valley. I didn't think much of the fence during the first few years of my travels; perhaps, I did not even notice it. One day, the fence began to take on a new life. Someone began painting that endless fence (hopefully, with some sort of spray machine), jet black. It took many trips to Rockford over many months before it appeared to be finished. And then, a few trips and perhaps a year later, it began to fade. It began to look like it needed tending. I wondered why anyone had felt compelled to paint that fence in the first place. Earlier this week, on the same stretch of road, the sun shone hard against a once-again jet-black stretch of fence. That fence is very important to somebody. I would even venture to say that someone loves it.

In recent days I have struggled with the realization that there are some things that I may never do. I can say with certainty that I will never dance the part of the Sugar Plum Fairy. Perhaps, though, one of my daughters, one day, will. We may never get to move to our farm. But our brick bungalow is cozy, healing, and hopeful. I may never get my doctorate as I have long hoped, but my oldest son is about to enter a PhD program.

So the tale spins on, not as I may have expected, but how it is supposed to be. There is grace in every day, beyond the pilling and the fresh paint, because we are here to love, and because we are loved.

We are the Roses in the Garden

(May 28, 2014)

My first winter as the mama of a sleepy newborn was also our first winter as homeowners, at least one of whom had enough time on her hands to dream of planting a garden. Our mail carrier trudged through six inches of fallen snow on a regular basis, bearing glorious nursery catalogs bursting with promise: nasturtiums, climbing sweet peas, heirloom tomatoes, and roses: hybrid tea, floribunda, and…"The Fairy."

"The Fairy" is a pink landscape rose which bears, even from late spring into early fall, meltaway masses of cheerful, 1940's kitchen-cabinet-pink miniature roses, worthy of the most precious princess. I had noticed "The Fairy" at the back entrance to my modest Elmhurst bungalow the previous summer, though I did not know its name. It came with the house, of course, and quickly became the plant which, to me, is closer to heaven than all the others put together. Finding its picture in a garden catalog, putting a name to its majesty, has allowed at least one Fairy rose to grace the yard in each of our homes…and there have been five!

I have learned during these recent days of chaos and anxiety to keep my rose gloves and garden basket close at hand. We are happiest, my youngest children and me, when we are outside. I have a chance at self-imposed therapy (in the form of pulling weeds or moving an unsuspecting plant to a new location) while the little ones bounce out the day's (or a wee bit of it, anyway) angst on the trampoline. Even five minutes leaves a tiny clearing where thistle had grown: a vision of what could be, and a pouring-in of peace to my weary soul.

It is almost always the same, though new favorites have joined the parade: perennial geraniums, sweet woodruff, lavender, hydrangeas, apple mint and chocolate mint, rosemary and thyme, among others, and all led, certainly, by "The Fairy." Each time, at each garden, I have tended my plants, fed them with (unthinkably stinky) fish emulsion, and watched them blossom. I have cut back their dead wood, mulched them for winter, and tried my best to rid them of black spot by gathering their fallen leaves. To others, my small patches may have looked like a lawnmower's "excuse me," but to me, they were certainly directly from heaven, because I loved them.

I like to think that the care I have given my Fairies and their garden companions has left them strong, resilient, and beautiful for their next "person." They have taught me many things along the way. The little icon of the sun in the garden mailer should have been enough to keep me from planting a Fairy in the shade of two evergreens, but I am the "learn-by-doing" sort. As deeply as I love my children, I am realizing as they grow that they are their own entities. They have lived, influenced by many, some before ever I knew them, and what they do is, ultimately up to them. I have held them, I have fed them, and I have tended their wounds. Like the Fairy, some have caused pain with their thorns, thorns that they must have for protection: protection from something that is so much bigger than I am.

I hope they know always that they have been deeply loved; that goes for the flowers and the children. When I visited one of my old houses, I was delighted to see the coral-colored climbing rose that I had planted years before blooming with pride, peeking through its barely recognizable white wood trellis, more stoic and lush than I had remembered. As my sleepy newborn embarks on a doctoral program across the country, I am sad because I know I can no longer protect him; there won't be much time left for pulling weeds while he jumps on the trampoline. Strong and beautiful, he is ready to join the parade with The Fairy. And I am ready to enjoy the breathtaking beauty as it unfolds before me.

Finding a Mystery

(June 11, 2014)

A small circle of metal took its place, among other random things, on the kitchen counter top. Robin had "found a mystery" when his big brother took him to town for his usual: single vanilla custard with M & M's, in a cup. What was it about the rusty washer that made Robin look twice, and, moreover, allowed him to see the magic within?

I think it was the same thing that I saw in my friend Kate some 25 years ago, and the same thing that is woven and breathed through the existence of every human being, aware or not, on a daily basis. It's wonder.

Kate, to me, seemed a whole and centered person; already on track, and successfully. We were two of a half dozen graduate students working for our professor, often together in a tiny office where our heady perfumes mixed together in a peppery mix to make us feel like nearly one being. My friend could read and write Braille, and she already had dozens of schemes for teaching and making a difference in the lives of children with visual impairments. She invited me to stay at her college apartment on the evenings when she was not there, and when the idea of my commute to my parents' house in dense evening fog or a blinding Chicago snowstorm caused me significant anxiety, which was quite often.

I had the key; I had the key which would reveal just a bit more about my friend, and which would add another layer to the wonder of this early-twenty-something person who, to me, remains a treasure to behold. There I was, alone, at Stone Bridge Apartments. I had survived the quizzical looks of the fellow peeking around the door of the adjacent apartment as I fumbled to work the lock. Inside the space, counters lined with what seemed like dozens of mason jars brimming with beans, rice, lentils, millet, and the like, and well worn vintage wicker chairs inviting my curious company, resembled nothing of a typical college habitat. Sparsely furnished and somehow fully equipped, Kate's apartment filled me with a strong sense of peace and comfort, and our friendship has offered a connection that has since carried us through the trials of early adulthood, parenting, impending midlife, and, to a greater degree, the opportunity to look within ourselves.

Someone once told me, in reference to life's journey, that you "get on the bus, and you get off where it stops." I take this to mean that we really don't know what our new days have to offer. We really don't know what is inside, outside, or within. Do we have a hand in making things happen?

As a little girl and, secretly even into my early adulthood, I often envisioned myself as someone else. What if I had been my next-door neighbor, or a Swedish dressmaker, a missionary, or the leader of a political campaign? Twenty-two-year-old me, listening to 10,000 Maniacs and holding the promise of the future, could not see nearly fifty-year-old me, still listening to 10,000 Maniacs, with still so many questions, so many unopened doors, but so many paths worn and traveled. And right now, in this moment, there brews a wonderful mystery around the bend, as the bus prepares for its next stop.

Every year, on the Saturday just after Halloween, Kate and I spend a highly anticipated day together; we have found favorite spots (in an unlikely town) to sit for coffee and to share what our years have had to offer. Our lives have generated different rhythms…Kate is up with the sun, and I prefer the calm of the late-night laundry room. It is rare that we have much contact between each Rockford rendezvous. There was a string of years where I showed up with a different foster baby in the backpack, or where Kate had taken on a director's position in a birth to three program, and this was the first either friend had heard of the other's latest endeavor. The very act of getting off the bus each year, anticipating the wonder, fuels the journey.

The scrap piece of metal that my spirited four-year-old rescued from the street sweeper represents, for him, something to come, something to anticipate, and something to hope for. The little spark that made it stand out in stark difference to the rest of what lay on the ground…that is the force that defines the exceptional friendship, the force that makes turning the corner to see what lies ahead, one of life's greatest offerings, indeed.

What's Important to You

(May 22, 2014)

I see it, even in the microcosm of the universe that makes up my own not-so-tidy little family. Our fourteen-year-old Chae Young actually tucked with premeditation one pant leg (covered in cat hair as it was) into her striped knee sock. "I know. I want it that way," was her retort when I brought it to her attention and suggested that she might want to fix her pants before she left for school. She also meant to wear her brother's outgrown Under Armour shirt inside out.

She likes it that way, and who am I to judge? Did you intend to leave those Oreo crumbs all along the side of your mouth? Just wondering; just making sure.

If Adrian doesn't have a white bowl with "a lot, a lot of white," there is often an issue. We no longer question it or try to switch it out. We offer a hot one from the dishwasher, or, when necessary, we do a quick hand wash to produce a white bowl. Though this may seem similar to a toddler's impulsive urge for control (Chae Young, for a time, needed the blue cup, or the pink one, or whichever was not actually available), it is in fact very, very, very different.

Dan was helping the two little boys set the table. I heard Adrian's high-pitched protest from outside the kitchen. This noise, of late, has come to mean that our little boy is escalating, and that he might need intervention if he isn't tended to right away. "I don't want the dirty fork!"

"Give it to Mom. She likes 'dirty forks.'" And I do. The dirty forks came up from the basement a few years ago, when I came to the realization that we might never use our "real silver" utensils if they remained in the fancy velvet and wooden keeper where they had been since 1990.

The silver forks remind me of something. I am drawn to them in their imperfection. Under the tarnished layers of rust and green, these forks hold a bit of mystery. They have a past, and they are strong, detailed, and brave. I think they remind me of the traumatized children that have been in my care. Their strength and resilience is evident, on a given day, beneath the anger, angst, and often-unexplainable behaviors. They are stoic beyond measure. And no matter how much effort we put into polishing these utensils, the tarnish returns from time to time, for it can never be completely wiped away.

In 1978, milk tasted much colder in the chocolate brown Tupperware cup than it did in the pea green, orange, or yellow one. I am not sure it elicited the same comfort for my brother or sister; perhaps it reminded them of something else. This brown cup reminded me of cookies and cake, and it made me happy.

"Your eyebrows are messy," I was once told by a dear girlfriend, one that was neatly put together on a regular basis. She was older than me, and I did look to her for direction and advice. I am pretty sure that she gave my eyebrows more thought than I ever had. Even today, I prefer to pull weeds from my garden than to pluck my eyebrows.

In a white bowl, a chocolate Tupperware cup, a real silver fork, and a one-pant-leg-in fashion statement…there is comfort and meaning for someone. The souvenir given by a lost love, the way someone made you feel safe, the memory of your belly hurting from laughter with your birth siblings…they are meaningful. They are worth celebrating, because they are important to you.

The Magic is Inside
(January 10, 2015)

When the boys were small, I spent hours knitting. I was shown how by a young mom who had also taught her two-year-old to operate a sewing machine. Jonathan was in kindergarten at the Waldorf school when I was part of a handwork group that met at various homes and did such things as drink coffee, share stories, and create as our little ones played quietly by our sides. Though my fanciest projects were simple mohair bunnies and beginner doll pants, the rhythm of the wooden needles brought great comfort and satisfaction and kept my hands as busy as my wandering mind. At some point, I left my natural fiber yarns, my patterns, and my sense of peace in a wooden basket.

My intentions were there. The blankets to fill the basket by the couch, the hats (one for each little niece and nephew), and the fair isle sweaters; all were nearly tangible.

We're going to get together for lunch after the holidays. I'll call you.

Coffee sounds great. Let's set a date for next week.

I really wanted to help you through your struggles, to hold you, to console you...only my own pain and grief kept getting in the way.

I really wanted to be able to hear you, to absorb the hit, but so many years of freezing cold have made me numb.

The old patterns are there, deep within. We increase the dose, things lighten up, and then the behaviors once again creep to the surface.

More than once, one of my foster children has returned, starry-eyed in anticipation yet peppered with angst and unnamed, indecipherable emotions, from a visit with mom or dad.

"I'm getting a big play kitchen and a car that really works as soon as I go back home!"

"Oh!"

The intention was certainly, unquestionably there. Stuff...life...got in the way.

During my Waldorf years, I taught a watercolor painting class for children at a dreamy little art studio in a space above my favorite coffee shop, the Starry Sky. The sweet smell of vanilla lattes and chai tea mingled with earthy aromas of clay and paint thinner to create a band of sustenance that must have sparked creativity and driven inspiration. A little girl once asked me if I was a witch. "Not a bad witch, a magical witch." I am not sure how I responded at the time, but I have never forgotten her question, the answer to which I only wish could be an emphatic, "yes!"

At some point in my life, there was a transition between the little child that spent her days taking care of her baby dolls, and the young tween on the brink of what her future held. I am pretty sure I remember a specific incident where my awareness of this difference was clear. I was at the mall, old enough for my mom to let me wander around alone for a while. The toy store, doll section (of course), was where I landed. In that moment of time, though, I no longer found the doll that cried real tears, the dolls that ate little packets of something that resembled Jell-o, or even the doll that danced ballet, the slightest bit desirable. What happened to the magic?

Though I had loved the song, "Puff, the Magic Dragon," for many years, it seemed to take on new meaning as I watched my baby boy grow to school age. I was afraid that without his lifelong friend (and I am completely aware that this could be interpreted in more ways than one), he may not be brave. I cried for him and for me, because the magic might slip away.

And perhaps some of it did. But it must be in there, still, taking on a different form, even as he works on his research, in the warmth of the California sun, on creating the feeling of "awe"; even as I spend my days on my hands and knees, washing indeterminate substances from the floor and holding writhing little bodies who so desperately need to be heard and understood.

I think it's still there. Just because life has gotten in the way, and because we don't feel it just as we did before, I am holding hope that one day, we can take a look behind us, and it may all make sense. I have picked up my knitting half a dozen times or more over the years, and each time I have had to consult "A Child's Book of Knitting" to once again learn to cast on, to knit, to purl, and to cast off. What is plain as day, though, is that "knitter's high," and the dreams that rush right back to steady my shaky hands. The feeling, the reason, is still there…somewhere…even if I have to keep starting over. And I think that's where the magic lies.

It always fills me up when the big kids are home for college breaks. Today, James is taking Michelle, his girlfriend of four years and a spritely burst of happiness and delight, if a human can be described as such, back to Loyola to finish her final semester. When she started school, Michelle joined a knitter's club. She would show me her knitting bag and her latest projects from time to time, and I would dream of the day when we would sit and do our handwork together. She is still at it, and her work has become quite complex, almost magical. And when I am ready, I know she will help me find that "knitter's high" once again, and maybe even teach me a cable stitch.

One Eye Missing
(January 19, 2015)

In my work as an early intervention therapist, I often found myself knocking hesitantly on the door of a home that I was visiting for the first time. It took a moment for me to catch my breath, to straighten my thoughts, and to knock with the confidence that I was ready, file in hand, to enter the home of another during what was certainly among the most vulnerable times in the family's life. Maybe the baby had been born early; maybe the little one was not meeting developmental milestones as expected; maybe there was a serious medical issue; maybe the family just wanted to "make sure the baby was okay." Part of my job was to use standardized tests and parent interviews to paint a picture of the child's areas of development. Part of my job was always to find something good, even on the most difficult day, because there was always something good to find.

Before we adopted Chae Young from Korea, we were presented with what I remember as a questionnaire of sorts. It was a checklist with the intent to match our family, according to our comfort level, with a child who was to have an adoption plan. On this paper were dozens of ailments and physical conditions, formed in two columns and resembling a grocery list. The potential adoptive parents were supposed to check the boxes next to the aliments or conditions that would be acceptable in their adopted child. One box said "one eye missing," and we did not check that box. We did check one or two boxes but, starry eyed as we may have been, we were "hoping" for a healthy child.

It wasn't enough to hold you, to talk to you, to carry you around, or even to offer you mother's milk. It wasn't even close. And neither eye was missing.

I looked for the cupcake. He had used all his might to squeeze the buttercream from the plastic bag, and now he wondered where it was. She had taken the best cupcake with the most frosting when I had looked away. She took it for herself, because she doesn't need anyone, except everyone. But she doesn't know how to tell them. She must have been wondering, "why didn't you save it for me?"

And then the tears flowed, and they never stopped.

My beautiful red-haired friend May rescues weathered or even battered furniture pieces and garage sale discards. In what may seem like the wave of her magic wand, she transforms a barnwood box into a wondrous, useful work of art. She can envision what others cannot; she sees it because she knows it is there.

I worked with Grace, a human angel if ever there was one, for many years, but before that she came to my home to help my child find his voice. She is able to find, perhaps in unconventional ways, methods to teach children to communicate. She knows how to find the bridge, and she has paved the path for so, so many, because she knew, in her soul, how to find the channel.

And then there is Mary, the one that helped me look inside myself, to show me that I had a job, and that I was equipped to handle it. She knew, though I sometimes do not believe.

Our friends adopted a little girl who is blind in one eye. I know that they did not check a box. And I know, as I am certain they do, that this precious girl is the one that was destined to be part of their family.

You tell all of your secrets (which may really be fantasies) to the man at the bus stop while burying them away from the one that rocked you, from the one that tried to console you, to quiet you, to comfort you.

There wasn't a box for it.

We were at the barn where the children ride horses, where all of my children have been welcomed on their good days and bad. There was a boy using sign language to communicate with his caregiver. On the way home from the barn, Chae Young remarked that she knew she could learn a lot from that boy, and how his jokes had made her laugh so hard. She knows how to find her heroes.

It's not exactly sitting together at the ballet or drinking tea, but it is closer than it was before.

Maybe our connection comes in realizing that we cannot be understood, in understanding that there actually is no understanding. Maybe our connection comes in knowing that the good is there, that we may not be able to meet halfway or even look one another in the eye on a tough day, but that we are here, together, just as we are supposed to be.

My Days of Awesometism, Dirty Georges, and an Extra Fox

(March 15, 2015)

We will need to find a spot for the Cat-in-the-Hat's hat. The on-the-way-to-the-basement wall is peppered with torn construction paper snowmen, noodles glued onto paper plates, and signs announcing such not-generally-followed anthems as, "gentle and kind, all the time." But there will be room for the Dr. Seuss-inspired artwork that made its way home via Adrian's backpack. I will find a special place and a bit of adhesive, and I will be forever reminded of the tiny celebrations that have brought us, for however long, our extra foxes.

It was one of the first books that Adrian picked up to read independently. In his daily challenges to make sense of his world, he must enjoy the routine and "sensible nonsense" contained within the pages of Dr. Seuss' ABC Book. He tilts his head to one side, his robust cheeks rise, and his grin puts the Cheshire cat to shame. I know, then, that he will speak the words of a middle aged philosopher, displaced into his seven-year-old body.

It was one of the mornings earlier this week when I tried to fit in one too many errands and arrived home just before Robin's bus was due to collect him. The heating contractor had parked his van at the top of the driveway, so we navigated the leftover ice patches and dirty puddles while hauling Target bags, an overstuffed diaper tote, and the baby carrier, which certainly weighs at least twice as much as the baby. We made it in the house and gathered Robin's things for school. I shuffled him out the door just as his bus arrived.

I thought the contractor had dropped some rags from his truck. As I looked closer, I saw two of Robin's precious Georges, in a flattened heap, complete with tire tread marks and dripping wet with the sludge of winter's aftermath. In my careless rush, I mustn't have noticed as they fell from the diaper bag. I went on with my business, because I had stuff to do. He loved them. He gave them to me to keep safe. And I didn't. I couldn't.

The baby came to us, the brother of one of our boys, after a lot of paperwork and two months of waiting for the State of Illinois to approve a sibling waiver to expand the capacity of our foster license. We are to care for the baby, to keep him safe, and to support the overall mission, in many ways, of keeping families together. Amazing, it is, to watch the blessings unfold with each sunrise. There must be nothing like being in the company of brothers.

I have three, actually four, extra foxes. In these gifts of days, I am able to walk through some of my most precious memories once again. The sweet blanket that was one of three or four things that came from the hospital with Robin can now safely swaddle this tiny new boy. I know, this may well be borrowed time, this chance for these boys to know one another, together in our home. So I am going to breathe it in, and I am going to remember the tiny beings that came to me before I knew how deeply I could love.

"I'm so happy that we had the air ducts cleaned!" This is not something that I would have expected to hear from any of my children, and certainly not from the seven-year-old. I am grateful; nonetheless, that someone shares my sentiment. With Adrian, there are extraordinary swings of angst, fear, and, even, aggression and, in the other direction, flashes of brilliance and uncanny cleverness to outsmart a university scholar on a good day. The days where the brilliance outweighs the angst; those are the days of, as James calls it, "awesometism." We relish those days, and we adore him. We are exhausted on all of the days, but he has brought us intangible things that we did not even know we needed.

Austin (our 25-year-old extra fox) reminded me of the day that we lost Adrian. Again, this was a day where there seemed to be more jobs than time. Adrian must have been three or four, and Robin was the carrier baby. Oh, the places we planned to go: the library, the eye doctor, McDonalds, even. In my frenzy to pack the bag and get out the door, I had lost track of my little boy. I asked Austin if he had seen Adrian. We hoped he had taken it upon himself to get in his car seat, as he often did; not this time. We each took one direction to circle the house. My path, my days as a foster mom, flashed through my head with an uncomfortable sense of doom. In the blink of an eye, something, everything, can change.

I have known many. Something happened, and things will never be just the same. We promised to keep you safe. And we really, truly believe we are trying our best. Which, every so often, may just not be enough.

I may even have been a little worried about the man from the blue house on the corner. He kept to himself and was seen walking his dog only occasionally. This day, though, he was my true hero as he walked toward our house with our smiling cherub. "He said he was going to McDonald's," the man from the blue house stated, as he smiled quietly with no hint of judgment. I wanted to hug the man, but instead I thanked him profusely. I'm sure Austin and I chorused whitewashed sighs of relief as we loaded into the car and ventured forth. From that day forward, I waved to the man from the blue house each time I saw him.

After a trip through the laundry, the Georges are nearly back to themselves. In some small way, though, they will never be just as they were before. None of us are, as we move through our days and emerge from our own battles. It is my job, now, to help my foxes find their way, to do my best to keep them safe, to embrace them through our mistakes, to love them through it all, and to celebrate the good and the challenges of every given day.

The Problem with Butter

(September 27, 2015)

To my great delight, she let me put a little bowl of milk in the garage for him. He wasn't allowed in the house, but he really was my kitty, at least for those couple of months, or for however long he continued to come around our ranch house on Varano Drive in the suburbs of St. Louis. My mom allowed me to feed him, and I called him Cinnamon Toast after what was, and still is, my best breakfast.

It's a glorious drive up north of Rockford; it's almost magical in the blaze of September's foliage. My one passenger has fallen asleep with her headphones in her ears, so I have no guilt for getting lost in my reveries as we combat miles of post-harvest cornstalks and hay bales reminiscent of an impressionist painting. If we stop making this journey to counseling, will it even make a difference? I wonder, but my soul would certainly miss the stillness of the country roads if we stayed behind. And maybe, just maybe, the healing is beginning.

The worst part about having cinnamon toast for breakfast is the butter.

"What's wrong with this butter? I can't get it to spread on my toast." Her look was one of anger, frustration, even blame. It's just butter. I love butter.

"Well, you could put it in the microwave to soften it a bit, or you can put it between two pieces of toast until it gets a little melty." She let out a sigh before I had even finished my words and kept rolling the butter along the toast with her knife.

"Or (and now I think she was getting mad), we can keep a stick in the butter dish in the cabinet so it's always ready."

We moved to Chicago in winter of my first grade year. I don't remember if Cinnamon Toast stopped coming around before we packed our suitcases, or if he would return to the garage, bewildered as he looked for his bowl of milk. I often wondered what happened to him, and I wondered if he wondered where the family that he once had, had gone. I wonder now, if my kids wonder about that sort of thing. There may be a new last name, but there is a lifetime of experiences and memories which cannot, which will not be forced away.

"Cart six's mom is here!" The voice of the emergency room receptionist reminded me of some sort of dart gun as it shot through the waiting room late on that Tuesday night. I had never before been called "Cart six's mom," but that is exactly what I became that night.

My child did not want me in the room with her.

"Have a seat, and the charge nurse will be out to speak with you." I chose a vinyl chair that blocked the emergency room door so I could not see the sick and wounded people as they entered. When I stretched out my legs, I noticed that in my haste to reach my daughter (who did not actually want me there) I had chosen one pink and one brown slipper. I was to spend the next seven or so hours waiting, wondering, and remaining on the other side of the door, with mismatched, though comfortable, slippers. My friend came to sit with me long into the morning. I wondered what the others thought as we tried to pass the time, and as our conversation led us, more than just once or twice, to laughter. How could we be laughing at a time like this? How could we not? Things are not always what we expect.

We have been at the farm for a month now. Foundation repairs and driveway gravel have replaced visions of a family room addition complete with woodstove. Even so, I am so grateful to be here. Each morning, I try my best to take a minute to look at the sunrise, to remind myself of the newness of the day and the anticipation of the gifts it might bear. I try to catch the evening sky, which often looks like smoothly-scooped sherbet or cotton candy spun with sparkly sugar. I know that, even on the darkest day, there are these reminders of what is here for us on this earth.

When the days are hard and long, when the harsh words are plentiful, the guilt, the anxiety, and the questions take over… the questions for which there are no answers.

My parents bought me a kitty named Ginger in the summer of 1973 or 1974. Ginger, unlike Cinnamon Toast, was an inside cat; she was the first in what would be a long line. There was Fifi Trixibelle, Coco, Rose, Fern, Snowball, Pearl, Semi Truck Driver Jeff, and now Juliet, who has just been caught licking the butter (which had been left out to soften). All were inside cats.

When the time is right, we are going to get some cats for the barn. One, I know, will be named Cinnamon Toast, to honor the one who has come before, to help me remember to celebrate the gifts of the moment, and to celebrate my favorite breakfast of all time…with butter.

Anywhere but Here: Learning from the Carrots

(July 13, 2016)

Tonight, I am a "pinhead" and a "tin can" many, many times over. He has spared me the worst of his verbal tirade, but this time the physical nature of his rage shook something inside of me as the shoe that he tried to throw at his brother hit me hard. The boys were mixing it up, and, as is too often how it goes, his anger had no mercy.

It's usually past dusk when I find my way outside to close the chicken door for the night. I don't like to force the chickens into the coop too early; I like to wait until they decide that they are ready to move up to their roosts and call it a night. This seems to be a common theme at the farm, that you just can't will things to happen. Whatever it is, it's going to unfold when the time has come.

Sometimes, when I look to the northwest at the setting sun, the colors of the sky are so vivid and bold, enchanting fires of orange and red, that I marvel at nature's artistry. When I turn and walk back toward the house, I am surrounded by soft misty blue, and I wonder how such a dichotomy can exist in this dusk sky.

On this night, though, I missed the sunset. To know that something has happened, that the time has come and gone...and to forever wonder what you have missed: that is part of the boundless beauty of this life. The things we can count on, what we take for granted, will rise and fall with the sun, ever the same, unless they are not.

When my daughter was born in Korea, her orphanage workers called her Chae Young, which, I learned, means "the color of the sky." When I thought of the sky, I had always envisioned a blue color, but now I see, and I know, that the richness of the color of the sky knows no boundaries and cannot be defined. My girl, you see, has shown me many, many colors: familiar shades of sky blue, but also colors that I did not know existed, and colors that are far more rich and beautiful than ones that I had ever seen before.

Though I have been gardening for twenty-five years, this is my first time growing carrots. I did my research through the winter, and planted the seeds in three rows. I was careful to respect the frost date, and I pushed the tiny seeds into the freshly turned soil, just as directed. When the carrot greens first poked through the soil, I felt very accomplished. I had read that carrots could be tricky to grow.

As they grew, I took care to thin my crop in areas where the carrots seemed to be growing too closely together. My family loves carrots, and soon there would be a great harvest, center stage at the dinner table.

My curiosity got the best of me. While I was picking the last few pods from my dwindling snap peas, I pulled up one of the carrots. Out came something that, according to Jonathan, resembled calamari more than a carrot. I had heard that carrots could be tricky to grow.... I pulled two more carrots that day, one more that looked like a squid and one that looked like...a carrot. I mustn't be very good at growing carrots.

More than once, she has told me that she would rather be anywhere but here. Here she was, though. Here we were. And through the brambles, we were growing. Almost in the way that I turned around and my little boys had grown to men, there was a different presence about her. She had caught me in tears, as the day's battles had gotten the best of me. She approached me, and something stirred. She stretched her arms around me, and there was something different in her touch: something new. She didn't say anything, but there wasn't anything I needed to hear.

It was getting late, and I was finally able to sit down at the kitchen table to gather my thoughts into words. She may or may not have noticed my hands on the keyboard as she approached. She wanted to tell me something. I told her I was working on my writing. She came back again, a few minutes later. It was something about 1/38 timing in percussion and playing cold turkey. I could barely keep my eyes open. I wondered what she was really talking about.

"Well, good night," she said. "I love you."

I could not remember a time when she had said those words before. I am not sure it matters if I miss a sunset, or if a day passes and I have not noticed the color of the sky.

I took a bite of that misshapen carrot, and it was crisp, sweet, and as tasty as any blue-ribbon winner at the fair. Tonight, I know that I don't want to be anywhere...but here.

■■■

James is far away, in Ireland, for his studies this semester. I doubt I had considered the feelings of my parents when I flew across the ocean thirty-some years ago to spend my own semester abroad. And with all I can, I hope that James is not missing me as I am missing him. He sends a photo every so often. In some of the pictures appears a tiny knitted chicken that I made in my Waldorf handwork group when James was a toddler. It somehow makes me feel better to see that chicken atop a mountain, near a gilded gate, or perched on a rock at a park. I know that James, many, many hours away, is not alone. When I think of what James went through as a child, when we knew not whether he would even survive, it is clear that a crown of thorns can, indeed, be a blessing. And I am content on this earth, under the Illinois sun, close to the soil in my backyard. counting the days until his return home.

We can forever wonder what is around the corner, or how our dreams will play out. We finally did find our farm, and Robin was not to be our caboose. Ihm Home Farm is the sixth house that our little...and not so little family has called home. Our hope is that here we will be planted for the rest of our days. The landscape is just beginning to take shape, and a few Fairy roses can be found, as long as one knows where to look for them. Joey is the twenty-third child to come into our home. I wonder if he will truly be the last. As I take in all that is around me, dare I ask, "Isn't that enough?"

When my chickens were first granted free range of the property, among their earliest garden casualties were, as I might have known, the first precious blooms on my Fairy rose at the edge of the herb garden. At this revelation, I had almost wondered if I should have kept the chickens confined. They must have known, though, what I was thinking, because it was not long before they discovered the merits of Stevia, basil, thyme, and many other garden delights, thus leaving the Fairy to once again grace us with her candy-pink sweetness.

I am happy to report that in addition to the white bowls, Adrian now also willingly eats from the melamine "Snap-Crackle-Pop" bowl. Just the other day, Robin grabbed a spoon as I was unloading the dishwasher. Before we moved, I had sent Michelle on a mission to Goodwill to replenish our spoon supply, and she brought back a wonderful eclectic assortment. The spoon that Robin chose was one of these. "I like this spoon," he said, as pointed to the fleur-de-lis pattern on the stainless steel handle. "It's the best one."

Last year, on my birthday, Jonathan sent me a clip of his music. He has picked up his trumpet to play again, from time to time. When I listened, the familiar notes of "Puff, the Magic Dragon" filled my ears and my soul. He had remembered; he had held onto the magic.

We do keep the butter dish in the pantry now, because you just never know when someone will need cinnamon toast. There was something about barn cats, or visiting cats like my childhood kitty, that I had not considered: they don't always stay around. We have had half a dozen cats come to the farm in the past year, and some have gone off, maybe reminiscent of when Adrian was going to make his way to McDonald's, only to be detoured by the man in the blue house. I have to find solace in knowing that all living things need their space and their freedom. They are ours, though, at least for a time.

I am learning to find happiness in my unrest and amid the unrest of others. These late summer sunsets are surreal, bright as Olympic gold, and as deep and meaningful as my teenage daughter's sincere embrace. The best place for the sunset is the view from behind the corn crib, as the patches of brightness reflect through the iron grid in contrast to the vine of miniature pumpkins that still creeps skyward. Last year, as I pulled brush from an old burn pile, I found a bright blue marble among dried sticks and leaves. It had to mean something. It fit perfectly atop a piece of what must have been a type of gate some decades before. I forgot about it, and the seasons made a full circle. Just yesterday, I was relieved to spend an hour in the garden after a challenging morning. I had forgotten about the blue marble, so it was a great surprise. It was a gentle reminder that things that we love truly do come back to us when we least expect them. I am going to keep looking for the blue marbles, and I am sure I will find some when I need them most.

OPENING WINDOWS TO THE PAST

As little children, it seems we are always anticipating that next birthday, that next milestone when we will finally hold the intangible. Those years and the moments held within must be more valuable than we realize, for it is the string of days, weeks, and years that lead us to who we are today. The cartwheels in the parking lot, the scraped knees, the places we spent our idle childhood hours, and the pieces of our pasts that meant something to us...all lead us to our true selves.

Looking back, we remember where we came from and what fed our souls through the years, and how we are still very much the same inside ourselves as always we have been. When we face our fears, as uncomfortable and unsettling as they may be, our past can help us heal. Sometimes, the most unlikely teacher brings us to just what we need, as my little boy did the day he led me to the train loft on a lazy afternoon.

In another story, a broken Christmas ornament becomes the parallel to a life that turned, unexpectedly, to take a very different path, one of despair but also of renewal. There is also a tale of butterscotch pudding, which reflects the complexity and the formative nature of our early relationships.

Through a children's prayer, there is a story of windows to the soul of another and the mysteries held within. My children have been through more than I may know in this lifetime. When we embrace all of who they are, even through the anger and the fear, we can better understand and even become part of their history, worn, but looking to tomorrow.

Nostalgia's Fallout: What Are You Afraid Of?

(July 24, 2014)

For me, there has always been an easy answer to that question. What am I afraid of? I am afraid that someone is going to throw up. I am afraid that someone is going to throw up on me. It is pretty easy for me to remember, vividly, who it was from each of my grade school classes that threw up, and under what circumstances. I can, even still, go into unsettling detail about those fateful days. In second grade, I had to go home to change because I had wet my pants when someone threw up.

The last time I threw up, I was fourteen. My revered cousin, Carrie, was visiting from St. Louis, and I was dreaming about a haunted house, late at night. Earlier, I had eaten lasagna for dinner. We went to a carnival, and I rode the monkey cages. Perhaps that combination had something to do with why I threw up. My brother threw up that night, too, but he probably doesn't remember.

My mom once told me that when I was a little girl, there was a ferris wheel incident where I thought it was raining, but someone was actually throwing up on me. I can trace my anxiety back no further than this.

As a mom to many children, I have learned to face this monster, armed with an ever present, fresh spray bottle of bleach water with the recommended ratio for germ control. In my early years of parenting, every contact was potential for an encounter with a stomach virus. I am not sure that I even identified this as anxiety, but it clearly was. These days, I prefer not to think about possibilities. I have gotten better; I no longer even pay attention to the three-second rule. Just eat it. You'll be fine. Or so I assure myself.

I am not afraid of cleaning throw-up; I must. I need to be sure that I sanitize; that I drive the badness away. It doesn't make me feel sick; at least, not if don't think about it. I guess I have actually become skilled at cleaning throw-up. Not long ago, something occurred to me. Perhaps it is not the actual throw-up that is my issue. When one of my dear ones complains of a stomach ache, hyper vigilance overcomes me. Check for the bleach water bottle, get a bucket, and make sure there is a towel to protect the furniture. Then wait. And, quite possibly, wait on edge as this germ weaves its way through the family. A whole week at the mercy of my greatest fear. But I won't get sick.

Here is what I am afraid of: the unknown. Waiting, listening in the night. If I know it's coming, I can't give way to sleep. There I sit in the dark, trying to control what I cannot. I don't know what's going to happen. And I cannot rest until I am certain that the beast is gone.

For some, the beast doesn't go away. Try as my child does, she cannot control the actions of those who have come before. She is, as am I in the throes of the flu, hyper vigilant to a degree that keeps her from embracing what is before her. She is afraid of the unknown. And it's pretty big, indeed.

Our neighbor's tree fell across our backyard last week. Remarkably, the sand pile had been unoccupied that late morning, and there was minimal damage. We have known for years that the tree would one day fall. Still, we planted and picked raspberries, made stick-and-mud pies, and pulled out weeds. We trusted. And we were okay.

How I wish my girl could know that in the end, it will be okay. Maybe, we all just need someone to tell us not to worry. We get through the sickness. We get to enjoy the freshness of an extra clean bathroom, and we feel liberated that the week is behind us. We have a wonderful ring of tree sections surrounding our sand pile now, making for excellent adventures of a new kind. The debris is gone, and we are now able to pick our raspberries again. And they are quite bountiful during this late July.

My Mom's Elvis
(September 10, 2014)

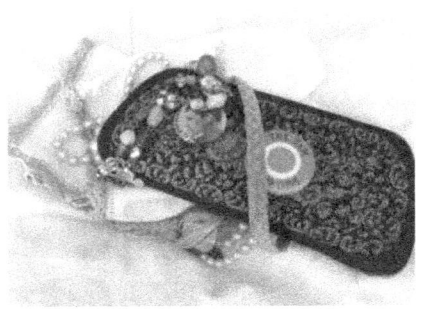

My little son needed someone to sit upstairs with him while he spent time in his train attic, which happens to be the loft in our bedroom. "Mom, why don't you go clean something?" I wondered what he was implying. It may have been that the neglected furniture needed a good dusting, or that it was time to match the odd socks that had been long since abandoned at the foot of the bed. More likely, though, he knew that I would need something to do to keep busy while he escaped to his berth where he alone was responsible for the movement, noise, and story lines that would follow. In his often-tumultuous world of autism, he knew that he could find safety and comfort at the controls of an eight-inch Metra. He needed to be by himself but not alone, and that is where I came in.

It had been years since I had given a thought to cleaning the top drawer of my dresser. Historically, that is where I have always kept things that seemingly had no other place; things that I probably didn't remember that I had; things that most likely I would never need; and things of which I certainly would not be able to recall the whereabouts. But things that, at some point in time, had great meaning to me.

My top drawer bears a certain smell, something reminiscent of my Saturday trips to Chicago's Flashy Trash and other thrift and vintage venues in the late 1980's where I spent idle afternoons searching for milk glass and marcasite, and of the heady aroma of incense...the Gonesh variety, sold at Record Revolution for $1.87 per pack during my days at the store, and still sold for that price when my family returned to DeKalb some years before the store closed its doors to end an era. As I sifted through the knotted strings of pearls, the handmade paper cards, and a wooden box that contained, among other things, a vial of holy water, I am pretty sure I heard music.

My boss at the record store once told me that "music bridges a lot of gaps." He was a wise man. For me, music allows me to cross bridges and filter thoughts that are otherwise too harsh to bear.

I spent many formative years of my childhood traveling through the states in our family's Coachmen motor home. My mom would blast Elvis music. This I did not like at all, but I could not protest. With all of her behind-the-scenes work as the camping mom, I am sure that she needed Elvis in much the same way as I need the Maniacs. I listen to my music when I am baking in my kitchen, when I am walking alone, and when I am in the garden for some self-imposed therapy. My children do not ask me to lower the volume. They must see the value of the Maniacs.

Through these recent years of reactivity, exhaustive behavior, and wiping stuff, I sometimes wonder if I have come close to losing part of who I used to be. Nearly closed for good in the drawer with the Jam buttons, the worn cotton friendship bracelet, and the mismatched earrings, I am still the same girl, though a bit jaded and twenty-some pounds heavier, that listened to the Maniacs for the first time, peering toward the blank canvas with hope for what was to come.

I am grateful that my older sons like my music.

My little boy climbed down from the train attic. He had returned the trains to the station, and his mission, for the moment, was complete. He didn't notice the sparkly earrings that I was wearing, nor was he aware of the gift that he had given me in that small hour.

Christmas Past

(December 27, 2014)

I love it a million times more than I did before it dropped from the tree. My vintage Humpty Dumpty ornament, with its sparkly blue-and-glitter nostalgia, shattered into a sorry sprawl of glass shards to signal the sure end of an already tearful Christmas holiday. For a short while, I saw myself in what used to be something whole, and not because of the mirror reflection. It had been a difficult few days. It has been a difficult year. We are all a little bit broken.

I cannot say that I know exactly how anybody feels. I can say, though, that there has been a sense of emptiness, a sense of confusion tied as a ribbon around the seemingly happy Christmas packages as I work to make sense of and manage what lies before me. I don't understand fully or know for sure, but I wonder if, at a truly primal level, my profound sadness at the end of an era heralds a vaguely similar sense of what could have been, what should have been for those mothers and fathers who were just not quite able to climb the wall to the other side. Though desperately they tried, there stood a barrier that was just too much to bear. Their time, as they had known it, ran out.

Last year when we went to visit Santa, the little boys refused to even enter the little cottage. I took their picture as they huddled sheepishly together at the bottom of the steps to the entry, terrified to be in the very vicinity of the jolly fellow. We did not attempt a visit this season.

We loved the tree. Adrian chose it on his first lap around the lot on Sycamore Road, and all agreed fervently that this was "the one." The unanimous consensus was, in itself, a Christmas miracle. The tree was smallish, with a top branch so wonderfully straight to provide the perfect perch for the old silver star. The "Christmas tree" smell was more powerful than any other in my memory. The little boys took turns caring for the tree, filling its reservoir with fresh water.

By Christmas night, it was clear that the tree's enchantment was nearing its earthly end. As the needles had fallen and the branches were now sparse, I could see the remnants of a dried leaf curled near the trunk. Perhaps it had fallen from a strong Oak tree, or maybe it blew from a raked pile during one of the blustery late fall winds, but it stood through Christmas like a tiny spy on the once glistening spruce that, today, stands its last battle. Still it held fast, it didn't fall, through the angst, through the tears, through the anxiety, through the uncertainty. It reveled in the moments of joy and clung to the proud backdrop to the family history which is held in the glass balls, woolen angels, and charismatic elves, all made radiant and royal amid the twinkling, sparkling iridescence of the Christmas lights.

Sometimes, I am that leaf, watching as an outsider as things unfold, things that are surely out of my control. I can't fix it or make it whole, ever again. I can only do my best to pick up the pieces. I'm not sure when or exactly where the Humpty Dumpty ornament came from; there are details of its history that we will never know. We were not its first home, though we were its last. I will love it still, through its brokenness, and I will know and remember its beauty and how delighted I was to place it high on the tree each year. We will open our doors to them, watch them, care for them, listen to them, pick them up, and, when the time comes, do our best to let them go with armfuls of hope and memories, and the knowledge of what it feels like to be cherished, so that they, too, may shine with a light so bright, so meaningful, and so like none other.

Butterscotch Pudding

(February 5, 2016)

My love for coffee began during my college years. I was a late-night studier, and this form of caffeine resonated better with my mother, who once found an open package of No-Doz (the one and only package of sorts that I ever possessed) in the top drawer of my dresser when I was home during winter break. Even the thought of my mom's reaction that day was enough to stave off any desire to try that again. If only I had such power over my children.

I was usually at Around-the-Clock (now a liquor store) or the Junction with a housemate or two, and I probably had more cream than coffee as I tried into the early morning hours to understand behavior theories and psychological "conditions."

Still trying, by the way.

Coffee, though, soon had me in a different stronghold: one that would represent calm, peace, contentment, and even hope. I picked up a black plastic carafe at a yard sale early in the summer before I took the graduate record exam. To ease my anxiety over the daunting prospect of this exam, which could certainly predict my future, I thought about coffee. I thought about the hazelnut coffee (black...no more cream) that would fill my second hand carafe as I walked along Lincoln Highway from my downtown apartment. Suddenly, the test was not quite so scary.

It's not just coffee; there are other things. With the birth of my third little son came some medical complications, and my mom, just days after losing her own mother, was by my side to support me and to help me get through a different kind of childbirth recovery than I had known with the older boys.

There I sat, probably on a pillow, alone at my kitchen table, made to feel better with the six or seven servings of homemade butterscotch pudding that Mom had made just for me. At age 31, I was allowed to eat right out of the Corningware serving bowl, and it was all for me. She knew how I liked it, refrigerated long enough for the top layer to be the perfect consistency, something that cannot be achieved in a snack pack. She knew. She's my mom. She knew that if I even saw the butterscotch pudding, I would start to feel better.

I have had children who are hardly children anymore come to my door, move into my house, and become, for however long, part of our family. They have lived a lifetime with others, not with me. They have learned what they need, who they are, and what they love, before they ever came through my doors. And I have no idea if they even like butterscotch pudding, much less if they like the homemade sort with the top layer or the grocery store brand.

I can still imagine the good coffee smell that would linger on my winter coat for hours after I left the Starry Sky. And I loved that coat, with the soft fake fur trim (the sales person promised that it was, indeed, fake fur) on the hood...until I discovered a tag, deep in the lining that stated boldly as if it were announcing a Broadway show: "FOX FUR." I never again felt the same way about that coat. I took it to a tailor who removed the fox fur, but it just didn't seem comfortable anymore. Even when it had the lingering smell of good coffee, it wasn't the same.

The Starry Sky closed its doors, and there has never been another coffee shop that held even close to the same charm.

My child got into an altercation with someone, and I found out days later. So many times I have tried explaining away behaviors, trying to enlighten others about trauma theory and how these behaviors have meaning. "The past is in the past...today is now..." I was told as I shared my thoughts on why this incident may have happened. But that cannot be true.

We are the collective of our own lives. We are coffee, butterscotch pudding, and the Starry Sky. We are what others have been to us. We mustn't forget that we all have a story, a long story, a mostly good story...our story. And that's the story we are supposed to have, fox fur and all.

I don't have the old carafe anymore, and I have learned to love a good breakfast blend at home with my Mr. Coffee. I could still eat at least half a dozen servings of butterscotch pudding, but only if my mom makes it for me.

Vagabond

(February 15, 2016)

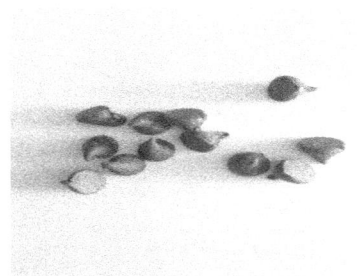

I doubt I ever noticed that there were apartments up there. If ever I had, I certainly didn't think about the people that lived there; I did not give a thought to who they were or to how they lived their lives.

"Angel of God, my guardian dear..."

This time, as I drove past the strip mall where the old Jungle building, now some sort of medical office, still stands, I did notice the line of windows at the top floor of the structure. In their streamlined sameness, they made me think of a submarine, or a cruise ship, where people boarded without knowing what their destinations would be.

"To whom His love commits me here..."

She still wore her school clothes, her pressed white blouse and navy trousers, when the social worker brought her to our door late that September afternoon. There was something in her eyes, a light that shone brightly then retreated to what seemed almost a haunting hollowness, something that she could hide in favor of the brightness when there was a threat, when she thought she was in danger, when she needed to be safe.

"Ever this night, be at my side…"

I could hear the girls forced conversation through the window. Their words followed the breeze as though they had no choice in the matter. "I like to read. What do you like to do?"

"I like to read."

The air on that early autumn day, with its freedom, handed the burden of getting to know yet another family, yet another set of rules, yet another new persona. It also handed the burden of digging her fears, her hurts, and her secrets just a little bit deeper.

She likes to read, because that is what she believes others think she should do. She wants others to think she is the same as them, though she has no intention of opening a book.

Within a matter of days, she figured out how we operate. She learned where things are and when people do things, and she learned the things that none of the others have ever needed to know. She even learned where I kept my secret stash of chocolate chips, the ones that I might need for emergency Michelle cookies. She, too, might need them for her own personal emergencies, or in case she thinks I have done something to her, in which case she may need to hurt me by taking what is mine, by taking what nobody else even knows is mine.

"To light and guard, …"

I loved living above the Hall of Cards. I may have stayed there forever if the semester hadn't ended, if I didn't have to student teach, and if I didn't need to know what was going to come next. Likely, there were many people that had no idea that anyone even lived upstairs from the shops downtown. My whole life, though, every beat of my daily rhythm, was up there, inside that apartment, in that space of time.

If we climbed on the roof of our apartment, we could peer through the windows of the mysterious building next door. At the top level of the structure, Bold letters, nearly as tall as me, sprawled across the windows that faced the street: V-A-G-A-B-O-N-D. Word had it that this had once been an antique store of sorts, and the owner had closed his doors and gone away, leaving the contents of his shop as an object of speculation for curious college students. I looked in wonder, fascinated by images of old caned chairs, depression glassware, and vintage cookie jars, each with a history of its own and a tale to tell, one which I would never have the privilege to know.

"To rule and guide…"

There is so much I will never know about her, about my child who came to me by way of sadness and pain. I can speculate, and I can learn bits and pieces if I look into her eyes when the light shines. When they are hollow and dark, though, I know that however deeply I try to understand, I will never see clearly into the window that houses her soul.

In the wake of her hyper vigilance, I, too, have become as such. In my quest for peace, calm, and healing for my child, I am now on edge. I need to make sure that darkness from days lived through windows of the past does not overcome the light of today.

She was a bit like a vagabond, moving from place to place over the years. The dust can settle now, though, as she is here, officially, to stay. It has been a while since she has flown about in a frenzy of anger and fear, packing her things and asking to move to a new home.

And now, thanks in part to books on tape and to an intensive reading program at the school, but mostly to her own tenacity, she actually does like to read. She knows now, too, to ask if she wants chocolate chips, because I will usually give some to her.

I can't see into those windows above the old strip mall by Greek Row, but I know that each is home to someone whose story began much before today.

"Amen."

Scratched and Dented

(April 24, 2016)

"Well, for one thing, I don't like that. You know what that usually means?"

I could only imagine what he was about to say, and I offered no answer to extend the conversation. He went on, as though he had been invited to answer, but he had not.

"Drugs. It usually means drugs, when people burn incense." My memory of his face is blurred, which might mean that I could not quite make out his features beyond the swirled smoke of Nag Champa, or, more likely, that I have blocked out his image as a function of his harsh assumption. My smoke alarms were mounted, my fire plan was neatly sketched, and my escape ladder was accessible. This Fire Marshall, though, was distracted by one of my comforts. He declared my home "fire-safe" for childcare, but not without sending me spinning into a category of potential drug addicts. I was good enough, maybe because I wasn't quite "bad" enough, but I wasn't whole.

The thoughts come so quickly, and leave just as fast. If I don't write them down, they may not be there when I need to let them go. I wonder where they are, the ones that have left, and what will happen if I don't release them, or more importantly, perhaps…what will happen if I do. Once, I felt them, so I knew them, but then they were gone.

It's fleeting, the time we have with these babies. Sometimes they are someone else's babies, but this does not mean that they were not here at all, once they are gone, gone home, and gone from my home. Truly, they never really leave the place deep inside.

"Is that your kid, I mean your real kid? Are you his real mom?"

Does he look like a real kid? Do I look like a real person?

As I settled my little boy in for his night's rest, I noticed the lace edge was beginning to separate from the soft blue fabric on the Peter Rabbit blanket, bought so many years before for my firstborn son. So, too, have the stitches that held the leather sole in place on the Hanna Andersson moccasins worn by nearly two decades of baby boys finally split to a state beyond repair. There's a certain comfort in holding these treasures, treasures to no one other than me, for the safe keeping of all the memories tucked within.

There was an estate sale in town on Friday. My desire to go was greater than my anxiety at bringing two boys, so off we went to explore someone else's history. A vintage cap gun happened to be the first thing that Adrian saw, and he was content to follow me through the tangle of vintage Pyrex, barrister bookcases, and garden hoses in exchange for the right to take it home. He wondered, but only for a moment, who lived here. I tried, though, as I always had, to figure that out. On a basement wall hung three Bauhaus posters. Two were the same, and all three were familiar, either because I had owned them during my college years, or because I had sold them at the record store where I once worked. I thought briefly of buying them. They were a bit torn at the corners but still displayed worthwhile memories from three decades past. I picked up what appeared to be pressboard puzzle pieces with an assortment of happy animals and smiling children, probably a treasure from the 1960's. When held together, the pieces formed a train engine with cars that displayed the name, "Jason." Perhaps Jason had been the Bauhaus fan. I wonder where Jason holds his memories.

It was a glorious Saturday, and we had spent most of the afternoon outside. Dan was working on the chicken run, and I had been planting my carrot and kale seeds. I heard, "What's for dinner, Mom?" at least three times before I went inside to figure that out. Just as I set the water to boil, I was drawn to the window as I saw a frantic parade of my family members running to the side yard. I wondered if one of the chickens had escaped from the tractor. "Kevin, call 9-1-1!" I knew from the urgency in Dan's voice that this was not about a chicken.

A car had taken out a telephone pole and flipped completely upside down in the field just east of our property. As I reached the slope on our hill, I could see a young woman crawling from the wreckage, crying that her boyfriend was inside. There, at the edge of the cornfield my eighteen-year-old Kevin was on the phone with the emergency operator while Dan found courage he did not know he had to urge the driver, pinned in the remains of the car, to try to stay calm.

Within minutes our quiet country road had been transformed into a blockade of lights, sirens, and helpers in uniform. I sat huddled with my younger children, one whose own early memory of a traumatic car accident stirred her old fears through sobs. We prayed for the man inside the car, and for all the brave helpers.

Once extracted from the vehicle, the man was able to walk to the ambulance. He was going to be okay.

The brightness of the sun, the streaks of lights on emergency vehicles, and my own destiny flashed before me late that Saturday afternoon. There are pieces of everyone…and everything…that we don't know. Sometimes we are presented with reasons to know and understand. The feelings, and our reactions, come from the memories, from what we have lived and experienced. Scratched, dented, ripping apart, imperfect as we all are, we are pieced together from our past.

I can light incense without thinking every time of that Fire Marshall. The image of what I saw this weekend, though, but the fear and the quiet triumph, will be with me for a long while. Maybe even forever.

■■

Looking back into my fears, the worst things may not seem quite as scary as they once did. Somehow, we got through the hard stuff; we made it to the other side. We are the same, but just maybe a little bit more of who we once were.

When we moved, we could not fit our bedroom furniture up the farmhouse staircase. We decided to part with the matched set that we had for a quarter century, and in place of the refurbished provincial dresser with brocade fabric, glass insets, and carved flower detail, my treasures are now stashed in my grandma's resurrected art deco bureau which had served a myriad of purposes over the years. Despite the loose handles and chipped inlaid wood, it is still quite serviceable and now holds itself with fresh reverence. I am reminded, in a waft of musty wonderfulness as I open the drawer each morning, of my pie-baking, story-telling, company-keeping grandmother, one who was surely a great teacher of the little things.

Once the glimmer of last year's holiday season had gone out, a package arrived from my dear soul friend, Mary. It was with a Christmas morning anticipation of childhood, though, that I peeked in the box to find a glorious new Humpty Dumpty ornament, bright and glittery, not necessarily to replace the broken memory but, as a step to healing, to honor, to remember, and to shine anew.

My mom sent four boxes of butterscotch pudding, the kind that you cook on the stove. I have yet to make them, for a couple different reasons. If I made a batch, maybe it wouldn't taste like my memory of the pudding that my mom used to make. It could change how I feel about butterscotch pudding. Or, the kids might eat it. But maybe that would be a good thing; they might like it, even if it doesn't come out just right. That, by itself, would fill my soul and make me happy.

My chocolate chips have mostly stopped disappearing. This is probably because, by now, it is known that the cookies or brownies that are made with them have a sweeter magic than a stolen handful or two. That's kind of what happens in a family. Many of us...blended together with all of what we have brought to the table, with all of our differences, can become something pretty good when we are mixed together.

We might have speculated, but we didn't really know how long Joey would be staying with us, or that he would be here with us, as part of our family, for the rest of our days. If he had moved on, if he had been returned home, he would certainly carry a part of us with him. And I would know that he, as had all the brothers before, had his turn with the beloved slippers and the Peter Rabbit blanket along his journey.

STRENGTH FOR THE JOURNEY

We anticipate, we hope, and we wait, because the moment is certainly coming. One day, it will be here. Then, we will look back, and perhaps at least have some clarity. In the mean time, we might expect anger, hostility, and things that we don't know about. This is the space between, where we must find the things to carry us along the way, to fuel us for the next step. It is the hint of sun, the unexpected act of kindness, and the hours stolen with a longtime friend, that promise us there will be brightness ahead, that make us believe we should hold fast to where we are.

Through stories of continued court dates that lead to more unrest and unsettled behaviors, through stories of inevitability, of standing up for what is right, of fighting for services for a child that nobody understands, we learn to do our best to let go of the extra stuff.

Perhaps our lack of awareness sometimes serves a purpose: to get us through to somewhere that we may otherwise not have had the strength to go. Once we see, once we understand, we know there is deep meaning in what has happened.

There are passages which tell of the complexity and fallout of deep trauma, the despair of concurrent psychiatric hospitalizations, and of the effects of these events that are shared by many. As the chaos is stirred to flow from one into others, we walk through our days, still holding our own sources of joy and inspiration, so that we may keep going. We reach in and we are pulled back over and again until one day, we can look behind to see that something has begun to shift. And that is where we find the hope, as we find the single bright bloom on an otherwise barren plant; that is where we find the strength that we need for this journey.

Hope

(March 21, 2014)

It snowed yesterday. This winter has been challenging, at best, even for the toughest of outdoor enthusiasts, one of which I certainly am not. I don't believe I was even aware of the fence yesterday as I traveled to Rockford for an important court hearing.

I thought it was going to be an important court hearing.

It seems someone forgot to file a paper and waited three days too long. That sort of thing happens. A child is made to wait…yet again. She hangs in that dark, unknown place; she has no choice but to remain at the mercy of the decision-makers. What is she waiting for? She doesn't really know. I am waiting for the same thing, whatever that may be. Sometimes, I am glad that all of this is not up to me. I am not in charge. I may (and do) tell my kids that I am in charge, but I sense that this is only as true as the task at hand.

So what can we expect until the next time? We don't know. Fear, anger, defiance, hostility, depression, and deep sadness are among the possibilities. But there is also hope. Hope and faith that what is in her best interest will, indeed, happen. Sometime.

Hope, too, for the promise of brighter days which must certainly be around the corner. Today's sun does its best to will away the heaping, debris-laden mounds of gray that remind us of the arduous winter. We sense that we have nearly endured it. We hear next week's prediction for, yet again, snow, but we hold on to the promise that we have felt the warmth of the spring sun. We know it is coming. We hope.

She hopes. She hopes for something, but she doesn't know what. She hopes to always remember who she is, how she has been and is loved, and to keep deep within a place inside of her, the notion that though things are not always as we wish them to be, there is always hope for tomorrow.

On Being a Stupid Shut-Up

(April 13, 2014)

We have had a string of good days. The sun has been spotted, and Spring begins to peep its eager greenness through the remainder of last year's leaves, long since abandoned by the rake.

It is always a good idea to go potty before you leave for school. As I suggested this to Adrian one morning last week, his response was this: "There he is! Hiding behind the tree! Fire on sector eleven!" Mom, you fool.

I am pretty sure that we Ihms march to the beat of a different drummer. And we do have many percussionists in the house. They are good at keeping rhythm, and many of them disarm angry feelings, loudly, and without discrimination. I am often called a "stupid shut-up," a name that has endeared itself to me over time. I will gladly be just that, a "stupid shut-up," as long as my voice is heard.

The following are words from a place deep inside of me, written last October as my little boy was about to transition from public school to a therapeutic day school. They carry grief, sadness, and a tiny spark of hope; hope that this turn in the already tumultuous journey would find the wind at our backs.

"A new bus. Another transition. My little boy is going to Hershey School, starting Monday. There have been so many waves of emotion and so many tears held back for something that I have known for a very long time. I have not been quiet in my stand, nor have I hesitated to tell others how passionately I felt that my son had deep needs that were not being addressed. March on to the next professional, who again questioned whether I was too quick to help my boy try to set the puzzle piece straight. The puzzle piece was warped, though, literally and figuratively. If you do not hear my voice, then I will keep going until I find someone that can.

I have been there plenty of times, on each side of the table. As a professional, I was a case of nerves more times than I can count. It's a hard thing to have to tell a parent news that they do not want to hear, but that they perhaps already know. I am so, so sorry if ever I acted with the slightest bit of disrespect. And it is a hard thing to receive such news…to be the aching parent unable to move your chair away from the industrial table that has served as the only barrier between you and the line of doctors and interns that have just told you that your son has a brain tumor. It is an awareness only born through (unfortunate) experience.

Curious, further, is the concept of selling your story, what you know in your heart to be true, when others are sure that you are either messed up and crazy or trying to find an excuse as to why your child behaves badly. This goes way beyond a crabby child who leaves the grocery shop without M&M's. I just need to say that I am so grateful to those who have lent an ear for all this time; to those of you who have said, 'that must be hard'; to those of you that have still been willing to help out with my children as my parents have moved away and my older sons have gone off to college; to those of you that have supported my calling (and I will always and forever WANT to continue to foster) and have NOT said, 'well, you signed up for this…' to those of you who have not judged me and have known that I would always want to act with the purest of intentions; and to those who understand me, and make me feel real, and sit with me for coffee, even making me feel like I mean something despite all of my brokenness (especially Dan, and the rest of you...you who know who you are).

I can say that I knew this was coming. I can say that I told MANY others, including teams of professionals (some of whom even scoffed at me...), that my son's needs were so great that he might one day need an alternative placement. We learn by doing, though, and I understand that. No regrets, just faith for brighter days ahead. Parents know their children, and it is a rare parent that would want such struggles for their child. I am grateful, also, as we travel this new road, that I have had my share of years to hear trumpet solos and to watch little league games.

As the seasons change and I reflect on how these last five years have brought many gifts (and a few injuries from flying objects and out-of-control children), I wonder if I will go back to my beloved job from which I 'retired' to care for this boy as a newborn. I wonder if I will have changed to be better able to see deep inside someone else, or whether I will be able to ask, 'what can I do for you?' instead of whipping out my checklist and declaring, 'I'm sorry, but I just don't see it.' Actually, I hope I never did that in the first place...

I guess I am looking forward to what lies ahead, though I have learned (thus far...for I've a long way yet to go) to embrace what I can from each day, and to let the rest go. I know that there are many more pieces to my little puzzle, and though the end result may not be as others perceive it should be, we will get there, one day."

Here's to all of the blooms of spring, summer, and beyond.

I'm Sick of Kangaroos

(April 28, 2014)

Yesterday, I took a few of the boys to the zoo. One of our first stops on our Sunday visit was to see the kangaroo joeys. While it was "the bird thing" (an emu, displaced, or perhaps not) that captured the attention of the little boys, I am pretty sure Kevin and I could have studied the curious patterns of the joeys for the extent of our stay.

"I'm sick of kangaroos." Those words found a place deep in my brain and only emerge from time to time, and when the task at hand is daunting. She was four, almost five, and I was her teacher. She had strawberry hair that fell in wispy ringlets around her perfectly rosy cheeks, and a sprawling batch of freckles. Her eyes were sparkling, a crystal blue-green, and she was the most gloriously beautiful child that had ever, to that point, graced the earth. Of that, I was sure. Something puzzling, though, about this fairy-like being, was her behavior. It was springtime when she steamed off the bus and exclaimed those fateful words as she spotted the zoo animal toys that were on the carpet for afternoon play time.

I don't think she was sick of kangaroos, specifically. I think she was just exhausted from the raging storm that continued, day after day, to barrage her insides, her outsides, and the walls around her. She was tired, and the kangaroos were the nearest victims.

It wasn't the greatest string of days. It seems a walnut found its way into the gear shift mechanism of my van. It would be likely that I may have accidentally dropped an almond in the car, among other things, but I do not generally eat walnuts while driving (only in brownies, and usually not in vehicles). I guess I was a bit relieved when the theory was revealed: a squirrel probably did it. Somehow, that made me feel better about having to pay fifty dollars.

Sometimes, like tonight, I am sick of the relentless verbal rant that comes my way as the regular bearer of news such as "it's time for your shower." Believe me, I would rather not remind this child, or any of the others, to take a shower. I would just like to find a nicer way for them to not be so stinky, but I cannot come up with one. It's not a battle worth fighting. It's okay. Hit me up. I can take it (tears streaming: mine, not hers). I would rather not let her see my emotion, for she has a greater depth of grief than any one person should have to bear in a lifetime. None of this is up to me.

Looking at the aftermath of my six-year-old's angst (overturned chair, broken seat, Lego shrapnel waiting to wound the innocent person that walks across the dining room), I think that he, too, must certainly be sick of kangaroos.

As I wallow through the halls of self-pity on this not-really-all-that-dreadful evening, I remind myself that I really do have something of a charmed life. And I am grateful for the kangaroo joeys exhibit at the zoo, which reminded me of my little red-haired friend, and made me think that decades later, she certainly must have found her ticket out. I know my children will do the same. Until then, I will be okay to eat brownies while they yell at me.

Completely Unaware

(August 24, 2014)

I really don't like cleaning James's room, because that means something: he is not home. This time, there lingers an unsettling heaviness, not just from the forgotten sock, balled in a barren corner since the last local tennis match. It's a sadness of parting, because my little sunshine boy has grown into an independent young man who has recently signed a lease, a lease which extends beyond the school year, to a house: a green house with vintage charm; the house where he will likely live this summer, and perhaps to the end of his college years. I never had to worry much about James's room. He was always tidy and, as a young boy, did not protest the Saturday morning house cleaning ritual, as did his siblings.

So I am cleaning what has been left behind, wishing my boy could go on one last latte run to toast the years of blessings of which I am reminded as I fill the under bed storage bins with golf balls, baseball trophies, and paraphernalia of a little boy's childhood. As I worked, Robin was at my side, uninterested in the certificates and ribbons, stacking the new-to-him wooden blocks that had been well-loved by my older boys. The fear which kept me from, to this point, allowing the younger set to play with the blocks is obvious: such a thing flying at someone's head could merit a trip to urgent care. I guess I never gave this a passing thought when I bought them in the early 1990's.

To me, the blocks are sweet, dear treasures from my most peaceful days of parenting. I must have ordered them from one of the natural baby catalogs that were, indeed, my sources of leisure reading during those sleepy days. I guess I never really looked at them, though. Now that I have, and now that my eyes have been opened, there is new meaning, and a higher (yes!) level of awareness.

The precious hedgehog, parked on a stump much like those in our newly arranged sand pile, and fancy in his snappy pink pants and wooden shoes, is certainly smoking something. I guess I just never noticed. I was focused on what I found enchanting: the shiny fruit, the dancing ladybugs, the playful gnomes, and the frolicking children. Yet I was completely unaware of the big picture.

I really do not like being caught unaware. I do not like, as probably nobody else does, being blindsided; learning of something that should have been shared. Sometimes, though, that ignorance must certainly serve a purpose. Perhaps I am just not aware. I guess it was the right time for me to really notice the little hedgehog happily indulging with a hookah. I have teenagers. I have had teenagers that are now grown men. And maybe there are some things that we are just not meant to realize…until we do.

Deep, unwavering love, the truest of friendships, and the goodness of one's spirit might be taken for granted until experience shows otherwise. I am not sure this means that we should live guardedly. Rather, I think I like the idea of giving all that I have, in each moment and with integrity, and never looking back. Each day, each moment, each breath…matters, as it is what we have, and what we are given. If I am pulled to awareness, I know that I have savored what was truly mine at the time.

All of my children, and all people, really, are unique. There are those that cross boundaries, those that may invoke a sense of anxiety or cause a gray hair…or many. And there are those that proceed to adulthood without seeming to step over a line. My lesson learned, today and for every day, is that I should take the days as they come, remembering that the actions of others really have nothing to do with me, and that I should strive to fill my soul with the positive energy that comes from living and loving, even if unaware of what is around the corner…or right in front of me.

Soul Emptying: Dreading Every Minute

(April 19, 2015)

When things are going well, you almost forget about it. In the brightest blue glaze of a surreal sky, frosted with opalescent pink clouds seeming to encapsulate you in their absolute wonder, the sun blinds the shadow and hides away the fear. Then, with a trigger so indiscernible as never to make itself known, there is a clash of pained spirits, a conflict among hurt children.

After at least a decade of pining (mostly to myself), I stopped combing my hair. Natural dreads, from what I understand, can take at least a year to upwards of three to look respectable (I suppose that means if you are of the camp that even thinks it is possible for dreads to be respectable). I am determined.

There is a time of confrontation: guilty, perhaps, of a tiny crime such as wearing her sister's best tank top without permission or eating the M&M's that were supposed to be for the Michelle cookies. Not even a big deal.

"I'm sorry. I shouldn't have done that. Do you forgive me?"

That's all it would take in the moment, but those words are elusive. The words that do come, though, are fast and fiery. They find a place deep inside where my soul opens up, and the insecurities from my own early days pour out, breaking down my strength through a cascade of grief. I can't let her see, for her own burdens would flatten a mountain. I can't expect her to be sorry, grateful, or even kind. Ever.

Maybe five or six sections of my hair now seem to have formed into baby dreads. There is one section in the back of my head that I don't even like looking at. I'm glad it's at the back of my head. There are some mornings when I wake unsure that I can face the day's offerings. I go about my business without making eye contact unless I really have to, burying myself in pancake batter, signing field trip permissions, and generally doing "things" to soften the tension and to move the minutes along until the angst (with the unknown…but not really…source) dissipates or the bus arrives, whichever comes first.

"I hate you. I hate you all. I don't want to be here. I never did, and I never will."

Never. At the times when she needs comfort the most, she becomes unreachable. What is she really looking for; what is she needing to know? Why does she have to open every new package of food, put her mark on each notebook, and stir the batter exactly the same number of times as the preschooler?

She needs to know. She needs to know that she matters just as much, again and again. Still, it's not enough.

Sometimes I think my hair is never really going to dread.

I am not giving up. And I am not giving up on her. I will continue to go to bat for her time and again, to try to explain her behaviors, to make excuses for why she took the teenager's I-pod or threatened to bury another child under the school.

I don't have to know what to say. There is nothing to say. I just have to keep going.

She is caught in a lie, and her deepest wounds open. She misses her family. She misses her life as it was before, however chaotic or unsafe. And she tries to match the chaos inside her own soul by inciting conflict in every arena. This I have learned firsthand.

I wonder why I can't ever be enough; why none of us can be enough; why nothing can ever be enough, except what cannot ever be.

We have been at it for a while now. Just as with the knots in my hair, I like to think that there really are the tiniest changes happening with every passing minute, changes that let her know that we are, indeed, going to stand by her, take care of her, and love her in our best way.

Forever.

The Rainbow's End

(August 4, 2015)

Last summer, I spent at least ten hours in my garden every week. It was the first time in all my years of gardening that when the leaves began to fall, the air turned cooler, and the blooms were mostly spent, I was able to put away my rose gloves and best weeder knowing that I had tended every square inch of this sacred space, and confident that, at least for now, my work here was done. This summer, with the anticipated move to our farmhouse, the addition of a new foster baby to our family, and our struggles with the demons of mental illness, I have spent less than ten collective hours on my knees among the thorns, weeds, and unmatched solace of Mother Nature.

Sometimes, when I am thinking too hard, I wonder why I love the great game of baseball. I look forward to listening to the radio every day, and I am secretly thankful for a late night west coast game or even a rain delay, for I know that this means more time to anticipate, more time for the chatter of broadcasters, and, perhaps, a little something to distract me, to soften my reality, hours into the night. At times I wonder, though, what it all means. What really is the point of following baseball, day after day, year after year? And then, I remember how much joy this pastime brings into my life, and I think that maybe it doesn't really have to mean anything at all to be worth something.

After a quarter century of parenting, I have earned an unenviable badge of honor: I have had two children in psychiatric hospitals at the same time for ten long days this July.

"Maybe if you were kinder to her…"

"Maybe if you were more firm with her…"

"She's so sweet, and so charming! I don't see the issues."

"Maybe if you just…"

Unless you have lived with a child with reactive attachment disorder, you really have no idea.

There are some thoughts that I won't let myself entertain. What would it be like? What would be missing? What would be lost? I can't think of what might be different or better, because there are no regrets.

"I'm never coming home. Don't call me; I'll call you. But I want my stuff."

Armed with the watered down remains of yesterday's latte and my Google map to the Chicago hospital, I know I am not ready. This is hard, hard stuff. There is no book about it. The pit in my stomach is not just because I, among the most nervous of drivers, have to travel the highway to meet my daughter for visiting hours.

I don't know what to expect from my little girl, my frightened child, who is now nearly an adult. What has she said? What has she yet to say? Will her words come from that hurt place in her heart, from the place that knows only how to say things to keep a safe distance from those who care for her? Will I once again feel the need to stand in my own defense as she casts, time and time again, the bitterest verbal stones? Can those first, early wounds ever really heal? Do these patterns, these ways of walling herself from those who love her best, come from multiple caregivers and the abrupt disruption of early relationships? Is this even worth wondering about?

There is no medication for reactive attachment disorder.

As she struggles to free herself from the pain inside, she knocks us down, time and again.

"She's a teenager."

"She's hormonal."

"Typical siblings."

Attempts at comfort by those who mean well. Yes, she is all of those. And that makes it even scarier, for her, and for us.

These ramps and arrows confuse me as I navigate into the city. So, too, do the messages that come from the lips of my child.

"Mom, I know I need to work on some things. I do miss you guys. I hope I can come home soon."

The storm seemed to set in to the rhythm of my steps as I made my way to the car. I braced myself for the drive home, which somehow did not seem nearly as daunting now that my visit was behind me. The sky was certainly ominous; it seemed I would be driving right into it. There was a great, bold flash of lightning against the stone gray sky, and just then the road curved to point me to clear skies. The rain was light, and though I was too distracted to look for it, I knew there must be a rainbow somewhere.

I know, too, that whether or not I can find meaning on a given day, there will be a day, nonetheless, and I can listen to the game on the radio. On that day, during that drive home, I listened to the Cubs win a great game.

Dan had taken some of the little kids on a bike ride, and I was able to steal forty-five minutes in the garden while the baby slept in his stroller. My Bonica roses had always been glorious in their midsummer bloom, welcoming guests to our home with their fragrance and sweetness. This year, though, there was just one lonely bloom in a thicket of thorns and dead wood. I had already packed my rose gloves for the farm, so I braved pruning them to a just a few inches with some old work gloves. My hands are sore, but I am hopeful the flowers will come back as before with new found strength.

And I know we are going to be okay.

Spinning: Through the Window

(February 29, 2016)

It's a Fun Fair. It's supposed to be fun.

Since we have moved to the farm, I think I have a new hobby: looking out my windows at the various Northern Illinois landscapes that surround me. The evening is the best time for this, no matter which direction I choose. The sunsets come in a palette of my best colors: pinks, golds, and oranges that range from the quietest warm to radiance of a physical nature. Sometimes, as I look to the west, I can see lights, too far to be coming from the neighbor's farm, mixing into the powdery sky, late into dusk, almost night.

The university buildings offer their light and energy of a different sort with my view to the east. I think of the students making their way back to their dorms after classes, and tolerating the season's final few icy winds along the trek. I can see the barren post-harvest fields through the grove of trees at the north end of our property; those that farm these fields must be, like me, eager for the promise of spring.

My mind races.

The windmills spin in the distance south and west of the farm. From this safe distance, they seem peaceful and purposeful. Up close, they are foreboding. They are scary, like the Fun Fair.

I don't like the Fun Fair. I am afraid of the Fun Fair. Windmills remind me of pinwheels, except for the fact that the person with the pinwheel has some control over when it spins. Control, that is, until the wind takes it. And then, it's no longer up to us. Pinwheels remind me of windmills, and then I think of the Fun Fair, and how it is not fun for everyone. When the first people thought of Fun Fairs, they didn't think of me, and how I would feel about the Fun Fair.

She seemed a bit disgruntled as she fumbled about the computer, looking for her headphones so she could listen to music while she did her homework. Her angst was the type that would certainly settle itself if nobody acknowledged the steam, which was a mere whistle relative to the fervently boiling kettles of the not too distant past. She found her headphones, returned to her seat at the computer, and announced that she was writing a personal narrative.

The flower boxes boasted their early autumn splendor in a royal array of green and purple kale, bold pansies rising to the warm sun, and miniature pumpkins and gourds for a touch of whimsy and to herald the winds of change. She never spoke of the pumpkins or the pansies, though. What she remembered was the sign in the yard of the quaint brick bungalow in the middle of Third Street, the sign which announced for all to see: FOR SALE.

Caught in my own anxiety and my hope that she would feel welcome, that she would like us, I didn't think of her, or of what she would think when she saw that sign. I didn't know if she liked Fun Fairs…or windmills…or pinwheels. Through her personal narrative that she wrote many years later, though, I learned that she saw that FOR SALE sign, and that she wondered if she would stay with this family, too, or if she would move on.

Here's the problem with most of these things: there's nowhere to put your fears.

And so we spin out, again and again, and we attend many Fun Fairs, even if they are not fun. Fun Fairs are chaotic, filled with indiscernible smells, unsettling noises, Bozo buckets, cake walks, and plastic prizes, a dollar a dozen. I can't volunteer at the Fun Fair. I will, though, bake something. I will make a cake for the cake walk.

As the storm passed through, it took with it some of our fears, at least for a time.

As it turns out, she likes the fun fair. And she seems to like us, too, though it may have taken some time. She likes the sunsets, the university town, and the fields of Northern Illinois.

Like the birds, fly free and retreat.

I can't understand what I didn't know in the first place, but I can look hard, in every direction, until I see you.

Inspiration taken from R.E.M., "Half a World Away"

• •

We don't really know what we're waiting for. I guess that's why we need strength for the journey.

Adrian still attends the therapeutic day school where he was placed after one month in public school kindergarten. This year, he moved to a classroom with older children. My fears had set in with this anticipated transition out of the primary age classroom where he had spent the last three years, with the very same, very dedicated and capable teacher. The staff has worked together, though, to keep the programs consistent, and our boy is doing fine with his equally dedicated and capable new teacher.

Two years ago, Adrian had more physical holds for out-of-control behavior than anyone else at the school. I wondered where he would go if he hadn't been able to stay there. Last year was better, though, and I no longer need to entertain the "what if's." At least, that is, not right now.

Looking back on these words, I can feel the force of my soul as I was on my knees, pleading for help and support for this little boy. Now, there isn't anyone that has spent a little time with Adrian who would question the depth of his needs. I must have had a lot to learn along the way.

Behaviors soften, or at least take a different form, as time goes along. Today, I had to call for service because "someone" may have put a golf ball in the exhaust pipe of the furnace. Forty dollars and half an hour later, the golf ball has been recovered...just in time for the coolest night of the season.

It's our journey, but we are probably not in charge of it. If we choose to step off the path, then that is the first step on the new path, which is still our path all the same.

Through the pain, the sadness, and the unwelcome surprises, we gather our strength in the company of those dear to us, the discovery of an egg in the nest box, and the celebratory late summer bouquet of flowers from a best friend.

Once my eyes have been opened, I may not be able to see, at least, not as I once did. Looking at the big picture may just be too much. The road is long. It's the little steps, one tired foot in front of the other, that take us where we really need to be. And we can always wear pink sparkly shoes, just to be a little bit fancy along the way.

That one crazy section at the back of my head that gave me such trouble is now my best dread. The swirling angst still visits on occasion, but time has carried us through a range of emotions, over and again, and again. New dreads are taking hold, strong, sometimes wild, often messy. I have gone a couple of times now to a stylist who has helped me out when the tangles have gotten out of control. Yesterday, I even got a cocklebur stuck in my hair. I didn't expect that. I'm not giving up. Not yet; not ever. I am guessing, too, that neither is my girl. But we know when we need to call for help.

I will never be finished with my garden work here at the farm. That's just fine, for when all of my little ones are grown and gone, tending what has been planted will give meaning and purpose to my hours in the sunset of my life.

Each day, though, right now, is enough.

It was with great relief that I learned that Robin's school does not hold a Fun Fair, but rather a Fall Festival which happens outside in the open fields and parking lot of the school grounds. This year, it was held outside, on a perfect early fall evening. The attractions included a little petting zoo, and there was even a chicken. As I watched Robin skip off to the playground with his equally energetic friend, I was truly content to be there.

Here at the farm, I have found plenty of places to put my fears. I can go to the front porch, to the little forest, or even to the chicken coop for just a little while...to unload a bit of the day's burden. My hope is that for years to come, others will find peace and healing in what this farm, and in what being part of a family, with all its shortcomings, has to offer.

Looking back through the struggles, the embarrassment, the confusion, and even the unthinkable, amid the joy and daily grace, it must be important to embrace it all, because it is our collective experiences, those parts together as one, that make us, in the end, whole.

BECAUSE THE END IS JUST THE BEGINNING

These days, we are contemplating whether to close our home to fostering. It would certainly signal the end of an era, but it would also herald the beginning of what is yet to come. We have experienced much together, yet there is much before us, much to tend, and much to keep us going. We forge ahead where the path may lead, and our stories continue as they are meant to be.

Foster Parenting 101
(January 24, 2016)

My first son slept "like a baby" from his very early days. As a well-rested young stay-at-home mom, I sometimes found myself making a bit of noise outside the nursery door by about nine in the morning, when I was ready for some company.

My second little boy did not follow this pattern, as he woke many times through the night for his first three years until, curiously, his baby brother, also prone to night waking, arrived.

I really didn't mind getting up with the babies. A mostly quiet house in the dark stillness of night offered a sense of peace, even serenity, which restored me much as if I had slept a full night.

I guess my little boys prepared me, but only in a small way, for the endless night wakings that were to come. Now, the imagined demons in the night reach their accusatory hands toward me, and anxiety speeds through my insides as I wonder, "Am I enough?"

The dull ache in the hip of my nearly half-century old frame gives me pause as I move to the room at the west end of our farmhouse, listening outside the nursery door. I am working hard at sleep training with this little one, because those every-two-hour wakings are no longer exactly enchanting. I had read Margaret Wise Brown's "Little Fur Family" (my miniature version bound in pretend fur) before putting him down tonight, and I am hoping he takes the mother bear's advice to sleep all night.

Other than possibly my little fur-bound volume, though, there is really no book for any of this.

Over the years, people have asked many questions and made plenty of statements about fostering. I am convinced that the vast majority of these questions and comments come from a place of curiosity, from well-intentioned people that are genuinely interested in our family. I have decided to share some of these questions, along with the responses that I have to offer.

"Are they yours?"

They are my heartbeat; they are my priority. They were born to another woman, and while they are with me, they are never completely mine, yet they are, without a doubt, my children.

"Why doesn't she live with her real parents?"

Many things relative to foster care are confidential. It is not up to me to disclose this kind of information to the lady in line next to me at the bagel shop, but I can give you an idea. As parents, we have much in common. We love our children, and we work hard every day to do our best for them. Sometimes, though, something happens...something unfortunate, something tragic, something unexpected. We may be just one "something" away from being unable to care for our own little ones.

"I could never give them back."

I was reading through some of my old college files the other day. Though the vision I had for myself twenty-seven years ago is similar today, there are some detours. I had seen myself pursuing higher education, with plans of fostering and adopting swirled together with one noble, starry-eyed wave of a magic wand, ending in a whole gaggle of little children. I never made it to the PhD. I did get the big family, but by no wave of a wand. Rather, through the grief and pain of terminated parental rights, abandoned babies, and lives overcome by addiction and mental illness. My family has also experienced the joy of working with birth parents whose children are returned home. We don't "give them back." We support them and love them as their fate is determined by the actions of others. And yes, it is hard, whatever the outcome, but there can also be indescribable, unfathomable joy, and that truly is magic.

"How many are you going to have?"

If I had a crystal ball, I don't think I would look. At least, not yet. No part of this is up to me. We spend our days, and a call comes about a baby sibling to our son. I wonder if I should pack up the bottles for good. With my older children on the brink of adult life, I know the richness of motherhood, and while I learn so much from others, I sometimes forget what I used to know.

"Doesn't this impact your marriage?"

Of course it does; however could it not? We are destined for this, just as all the stars are numbered, there is reason and meaning behind all of our connections. We could not do this alone. Times are best when we work together. After twenty-five years of marriage, we have learned ways to support one another. Dan can tell when I have had too much; he knows when I am on the verge of tears, and my arms are sore from holding a writhing eight-year-old. He gently takes over, and I can spend some mindless minutes peeling carrots. I know, too, that if he slips upstairs to play his keyboard for a little while, this time will fill his soul so that he may be energized for the next round.

"Don't you worry how this will affect your other kids?

I worry that my two-year-old will hear words that I hope he never repeats. I worry that my daughter will learn certain things well before she should. I worry that my children will see me cry, or that they will feel like I don't have time for them. I even worried about the cat when she was the subject of a bad experiment. Then I see the collective joy of my little son and his baby brother as they chase each other around the kitchen. I see the little sparkles shared between my girls as they talk about things that girls talk about. I see in my grown sons a sense of compassion and understanding that can only come from having experienced this side of life.

We do this, plain and simple, because that is why we are here.

Today was a sunny Sunday, close to thirty degrees, and I felt only slightly guilty for calling an officer to help me install a car seat for our one-year-old. I waited in my van outside the police station, and as he approached, I noticed that he looked slightly familiar. I wondered if he was one of the many officers who had come to the scene during one of the four times this year we had to call for help for an out-of-control child. He had done this many times before. He flipped the seat over a couple times, adjusted a few latches, gave me some safety tips, and gave the car seat a final tug. At one point, I looked sharply at this young policeman, beckoning him to pull up the details to my story. He didn't. He did his job. He was pleasant, kind, and unassuming toward the almost grandmotherly woman that needed help with the car seat for her baby.

There really are no answers to these questions. We do what we do because out of all of this brokenness and sadness, there is a light. I have seen it. There is another day, another sun, and another chance for hope and healing.

There is, indeed, another story to be written.

And for now, sleep peacefully, my little one.

ABOUT THE AUTHOR

Patty Ihm, a mother to many, lives on a farmette in Northern Illinois with her husband, Dan, their children who have not yet left the nest, and the strong memories of those that have. She spends her days tending her flock of chickens and children, working in the garden, drinking coffee, and listening to baseball on the radio. As a teacher, early intervention therapist, and foster/adoptive parent, Patty is an activist for children and families. She is grateful for those near and far that help her find meaning and who, along with teachers from days gone by, have encouraged her to put pen to paper with the intention to share the simplicity and emotionally of the hope and reverence to be found in every day.